Stoic Wisdom for Everyday Life

Thriving in Turbulent Times

Nikos Alexandros

© **Copyright 2024 - All rights reserved.**

The content contained within this book may not be reproduced, duplicated or transmitted without direct written permission from the author or the publisher.

Under no circumstances will any blame or legal responsibility be held against the publisher, or author, for any damages, reparation, or monetary loss due to the information contained within this book, either directly or indirectly.

Legal Notice:

This book is copyright protected. It is only for personal use. You cannot amend, distribute, sell, use, quote or paraphrase any part, or the content within this book, without the consent of the author or publisher.

Disclaimer Notice:

Please note the information contained within this document is for educational and entertainment purposes only. All effort has been executed to present accurate, up to date, reliable, complete information. No warranties of any kind are declared or implied. Readers acknowledge that the author is not engaged in the rendering of legal, financial, medical or professional advice. The content within this book has been derived from various sources. Please consult a licensed professional before attempting any techniques outlined in this book.

By reading this document, the reader agrees that under no circumstances is the author responsible for any losses, direct or indirect, that are incurred as a result of the use of the information contained within this document, including, but not limited to, errors, omissions, or inaccuracies.

Table of Contents

INTRODUCTION 1
    THE CENTRAL TENETS OF STOICISM 3

CHAPTER 1: THE STOIC MINDSET 5
    EXPLORING LIMITING BELIEFS 6
        Questions to Challenge Limiting Beliefs 9
    DEVELOPING A STOIC MINDSET IN THE WORKPLACE 11
        Cultivating a Stoic Mindset 12
    ROBERT: EMBRACING CHALLENGES 14

CHAPTER 2: SELF-REFLECTION AND MEDITATION 17
    THE POWER OF SELF-REFLECTION 18
    REFLECTING ON CHALLENGES 20
    INCORPORATING MEDITATION INTO YOUR DAILY ROUTINE 23
        More Techniques for Mindful Introspection 25
    MARION: GAINING A FRESH PERSPECTIVE 26

CHAPTER 3: RESILIENCE IN THE FACE OF ADVERSITY 29
    SEEKING ANSWERS FROM WITHIN 30
    BUILDING EMOTIONAL RESILIENCE 32
        Journaling and Emotional Awareness 32
        Focusing on the Controllable and Setting Realistic Goals 33
        Challenging Negativity and Affirming Positivity 33
        Practicing Gratitude 34
        Self-Compassion and Forgiveness 34
        Prioritizing Self-Care 35
        Maintaining a Social Support System 35
        Rediscovering Passions, Hobbies, and Interests 35
        Establishing a Routine and Cultivating Adaptability 36
    CULTIVATING INNER STRENGTH 36
        Developing Assertiveness, Courage, and Empathy 37
        Persistence and Grit 37
        Humor and Lightheartedness 37
        Contributions to the Community 38
    OLIVER: FOSTERING RESILIENCE 38

CHAPTER 4: FINDING MEANING AND PURPOSE 41

IDENTIFYING CORE VALUES 42
SETTING MEANINGFUL GOALS 44
   Setting Goals Based on Core Values 44
CREATING A PERSONAL MISSION STATEMENT 45
   Step 1: Reflecting on Core Values 46
   Step 2: Identifying Strengths and Limiting Beliefs 47
   Step 3: Exploring Passions and Interests 47
   Step 4: Drafting a Mission Statement 47
   Step 5: Practicing Affirmations and Mindfulness 48
   Step 6: Reviewing Your Mission Statement and Embracing Adaptability 48
MORRIS: FINDING A NEW LEASE ON LIFE 48

CHAPTER 5: VIRTUE AS THE HIGHEST GOOD 51

ETHICAL CONSIDERATIONS 52
UNDERSTANDING STOIC VIRTUE ETHICS 53
   Wisdom 54
   Courage 54
   Justice 54
   Moderation 54
APPLYING VIRTUE TO EVERYDAY CHOICES 55
   Reflecting on Values and Intentions 57
   Practicing Mindfulness and Discussing Virtue Ethics 57
   Creating Virtue-Based Habits 57
SARAH: EMBRACING FAIRNESS WITH INTEGRITY 58

CHAPTER 6: MANAGING ANGER AND NEGATIVE EMOTIONS 61

EMMA'S WORKPLACE CHALLENGES 62
STRATEGIES FOR EMOTIONAL SELF-CONTROL 62
   Setting Realistic Expectations 63
   Developing Emotional Intelligence 64
   Utilizing Stoic Affirmations 64
   Engaging in Cognitive Restructuring 64
EMMA: INITIATING CHANGE 65
EMMA'S RELATIONSHIP STRUGGLES 67
TECHNIQUES FOR MANAGING ANGER AND NEGATIVE EMOTIONS 67
   Progressive Muscle Relaxation 68
   Recontextualization 70
   Other Techniques for Managing Anger and Negativity 70
EMMA: FORGING A NEW PATH 73

CHAPTER 7: DEALING WITH CHANGE AND TRANSITION 77

EMBRACING CHANGE 78
PRACTICAL MEASURES FOR NAVIGATING TRANSITIONS 79
   Adopting a Stoic Mindset 79

Setting Expectations and Creating an Action Plan 80
Communicating Effectively 80
Building a Support System and Prioritizing Self-Care 80
Staying Flexible and Exploring New Perspectives 81
Celebrating Victories and Maintaining Positivity 81
MIA: ADAPTING TO A NEW LIFE 82

CHAPTER 8: FINDING CONTENTMENT AND INNER PEACE 85

THE PURSUIT OF "EUDAIMONIA" 86
PRACTICES FOR FINDING CONTENTMENT 87
CULTIVATING INNER PEACE 89
Mindfulness Meditation and Practices 90
Digital Detox 91
Affirmations and Boundaries 91
SAM: OPEN TO NEW POSSIBILITIES 92

CHAPTER 9: STOIC RELATIONSHIPS 95

APPLYING STOIC PRINCIPLES TO RELATIONSHIPS 96
STRATEGIES FOR IMPROVING COMMUNICATION AND EMPATHY 99
Active Listening 99
Avoiding Prejudgment 100
Putting Yourself in Others' Shoes 101
THE BAND: IMPROVED DYNAMICS AND PRESERVING A HARMONIOUS COLLABORATION 101

CHAPTER 10: STOICISM IN THE MODERN WORLD 103

INTEGRATING STOIC PRACTICES INTO EVERYDAY ROUTINES 104
Cognitive Restructuring and Positive Reinforcement 105
Mindfulness-Based Stress Reduction 105
Behavioral Activation 105
Problem-Solving Skills 106
Prospective Retrospection 106
Graded Exposure 106
TIM: BEING HIS BEST SELF 107

CONCLUSION 109

TIPS FOR CONTINUED STOIC GROWTH 110
Morning Meditation and Contemplation 111
Positive Affirmations 111
Daily Reflection and Self-Examination 111
Moment of Mindful Pause 111
Mindful Eating and Appreciation for Simple Pleasures 112
"Premeditatio Malorum" (Preparation for Adversity) 112
Digital Detox and Detachment From External Things 112
Kindness, Empathy, and Practicing Virtue in Relationships 112

Random Acts of Virtue	*113*
Stoic Reading	*113*
Nightly Gratitude	*113*
AUTHOR BIO	**115**
REFERENCES	**117**

Introduction

The best way to treat obstacles is to use them as stepping-stones. Laugh at them, tread on them, and let them lead you to something better. –Chrysippus *(In J. Christoph, 2009)*

Five years ago, my house burned down.

After the local authorities arrived on the scene to put out the fire and inspect the damage, it was determined to have been caused by a stray cigarette butt setting alight a small gas leak, which had been the inevitable result of a heating system overburdened by the demands of a harsh winter. My own first awareness of the blaze was when my partner and I were roused from our sleep in the middle of the night by the smell of thick smoke and burning wood. Most of my many treasured possessions were destroyed in the fire, and even the two of us only barely escaped with our lives. Not long after the incident, my partner and I split up, and not in an amicable manner. Our mutual friends mostly took her side, and my own social circles dwindled as a result.

In the span of a few weeks, my life had been completely overturned, and I was in a turbulent state of mind, with very few resources left to my name or good friends to turn to for solace. I was open to any path that would lead me back to a more stable, comfortable lifestyle. This was when I happened upon the philosophies of Zeno of Citium.

Zeno of Citium was no stranger to dramatic upheavals in life. While working as a merchant selling dyes, he was shipwrecked during a voyage from Phoenicia to Piraeus, the main port of Athens at the time. Although he survived, much of his earthly wealth (and, as such, his livelihood at the time) was lost to the Aegean Sea.

Zeno turned to philosophy in the search for a way forward from his tragic loss. After a fortuitous meeting with a philosopher named Crates of Thebes, he began to study various schools of philosophy, from the Cynics to the Megarians. From these, he devised and then taught his own brand of philosophy in a public walkway in Athens known as the *Stoa Poikile* ("Painted Portico"). Those who congregated there to listen to his teachings would come to be known as "Stoics," which is how his key philosophy of "Stoicism" got its name.

Zeno and the other premier practitioners of Stoicism, such as Seneca, Epictetus, and Marcus Aurelius, all lived during a time that was far simpler than ours, with far less knowledge about the workings of our world, and far fewer troubles to juggle because of it. So, one would be justified in asking: What could they possibly have to teach us that is relevant to this day?

As it so happens, and as I discovered five years ago in my own search for consolation and security, the tenets of Stoicism are evergreen; they relate to overcoming struggles that have remained unchanged in essence over time. Zeno couldn't have burned his house down with a stray cigarette and a gas leak, but when he lost his possessions at sea, and when I lost mine in the fire, we both felt the same kind of emptiness and devastation that Stoicism can be used to overcome.

Today, I once again live comfortably, at peace with myself and the people I now associate with. A large part of this change in my fortunes can be attributed to the lessons I learned from putting the philosophy of Stoicism into practice. However, it can be overwhelming at first to convert the pearls of wisdom and musings from the likes of Marcus Aurelius and Epictetus into something actionable in this day and age. The purpose of this book is to ease this particular translation for you— to connect the dots from the ancient philosophy and theory to modern practical applications, backed by relevant findings from modern psychologists, that can benefit your own life.

The Central Tenets of Stoicism

We cannot choose our external circumstances, but we can always choose how we respond to them. —Epictetus

Stoicism can be summed up by the above quote. The fundamental idea behind it is therefore this: *You are responsible for your own behavior.* No matter what happens to you, you can choose to react virtuously and live prosperously in accordance with your nature as a person. On the other hand, if you don't choose to act virtuously, there's no passing the buck either: The consequences of your actions are yours to be held accountable for. This can be both an empowering and a sobering maxim to live by, but it is ultimately a virtuous one.

The central tenets of Stoicism are as follows:

- You can't always control external events that act on you, but you can always control how you react to those circumstances. As such, a great deal of wisdom lies in understanding what you *can* control and what you *cannot*—and focusing on the former.

- The only true good is virtue, because it is good regardless of the context. While external qualities such as good health, wealth and pleasure can lead you astray in the wrong circumstances, acting virtuously is always positive. The Stoics argued that there are four cardinal virtues from which all other virtues derive: courage, justice, moderation, and wisdom.

- Human beings are innately able to reason, which means you can apply rational thinking to live in a way that is good. It follows, then, that you are innately capable of virtue. By choosing to act in a virtuous way, you live according to your nature and achieve a state of flourishing, or *eudaimonia.*

Another way of looking at Stoicism is that it enables you to have a better understanding of the agency you have over your life. As such, it can be argued that Stoicism has never been more relevant to modern life. After all, the modern world seems constantly intent on taking your agency away from you.

At any given moment, a thousand burdens and obligations could be pressing down on you at once. Multiple people, activities, and media sources vie for your attention, distracting you and making you feel like you never have enough time for all the things you want to do. This can cause you to act impulsively and quickly, without thinking through the consequences or considering what the virtuous thing to do is. Your rationality is then stripped away from you, which leads you to unwittingly make bad decisions and adds to a growing sense of stress and unfulfillment. Stoicism is the balm to these ills; it offers a chance for the calm reflection that modern life sorely lacks.

In this book, the teachings of the ancient Stoics will be applied to life in the modern world, focusing on practical strategies and tools for living according to Stoic principles in the 21st century. The writings of the Roman emperor Marcus Aurelius will be blended with the insights of modern psychology. The wisdom of ancient senators like Seneca and the moderation of the slave-turned-philosopher Epictetus will intermingle with advances in cognitive behavioral therapy (CBT).

This will be done by way of personal stories that illustrate these principles in practice. Whether you are facing turbulent times at your workplace or at home, due to the actions of other people or due to acts of nature, the trials overcome in these stories will likely contain something that resonates with you.

As you observe how the people in the following chapters use the virtues of Stoicism to overcome their own troubles, think about how their behavior could apply to circumstances more familiar to you, and how you can incorporate similar actions into your daily life. The primary goal of this book is to provide you with a toolkit of strategies, inspired by the stories of these people, that will enable you to incorporate Stoic principles into your daily living. It is my hope that the learning you take away from this book will help you strive toward an ideal Stoic life that works best for you.

Chapter 1:

The Stoic Mindset

He suffers more than necessary, who suffers before it is necessary. –Seneca

The concept of suffering more than necessary before it is necessary reflects on the importance of managing how we respond to challenges. A key part of this response is how one goes about deciding on the mindset that drives the decision. In this chapter, we will explore what it means to have a Stoic mindset, why such a mindset can contribute to a life with more benefits and less suffering, and how one can develop it.

Such a mindset can be of great use when dealing with workplace stress, for instance, as can be seen in the example of Robert below. By cultivating resilience with the help of Stoicism, Robert was able to address the difficulties he faced at work with a rational and measured approach, thereby avoiding unnecessary suffering.

Robert was a seasoned middle-level manager at a prominent international banking firm when he found himself navigating a shift in the landscape within the organization that would prove to be a challenge. Having successfully led a team of 20 across various locations around the globe, Robert found himself facing significant hurdles following a series of senior management changes and restructuring initiatives.

The aftermath of the most recent of many redundancy programs had dramatically reshaped Robert's team by, among other things, halving its size. In addition, a new layer of reporting had been introduced into the dynamic between Robert and his latest manager, creating an organizational structure that was perceived to be top-heavy. Lower-level employees now found themselves shouldering the responsibilities of multiple departed colleagues, leading to a noticeable decline in both the standards of their performance and their motivation as a team.

Compounding the issue was Robert's strained relationship with his new manager. Due to the manager's affinity for political maneuvering, he failed to provide the necessary support whenever Robert encountered challenges. Credit for Robert's hard work was claimed by his manager, and essential discussions on controversial topics were avoided altogether. This dynamic left Robert feeling stressed, disempowered, and indirectly demoted within the organization. During a particularly trying meeting, Robert found himself and his team implicitly blamed for a recent error; when he tried to defend his actions as well as theirs, he sensed that he was being considered "difficult," and felt the beginnings of a "clash of personalities" with one of the other, more senior managers in the hierarchy of their organization.

As a result of these challenges, Robert's own motivation dwindled, and his promising career trajectory seemed to have hit a roadblock. Frustrated and with little hope of promotion within his current role, Robert initiated a job search outside the organization, driven by the desire for a more supportive professional environment as well as a new working situation that offered better potential for his own career growth. This in turn led him to feel even more demotivated to continue with his work at his current firm.

Exploring Limiting Beliefs

If you are pained by any external thing, it is not this thing that disturbs you, but your own judgment about it. And it is in your power to wipe out this judgment now.
—Marcus Aurelius

What Robert was feeling at the onset of his challenges were what are called "limiting beliefs." Simply put, these are beliefs you can have about yourself that limit the potential of what you can achieve. Often negative and never helpful, limiting beliefs in their simplest form can look like the following: *I can't do anything right. Everything seems to backfire. My job/relationship/life is falling apart.*

These beliefs are limiting because, on some level, they let you off the hook. They are definitive, and don't allow for the possibility of changing things for the better—after all, why even try to succeed if you can't do anything right? Thoughts like these offer no constructive criticism or path toward personal growth, and are deeply demotivating and uncomfortable. If you're in the habit of holding limiting beliefs about yourself, this will affect your confidence and emotional well-being.

Limiting beliefs are unfair to you because they are not entirely true in their reductive view of matters. Let's say you believe you're bad at your job. Any job contains various responsibilities and multiple facets, and it's likely that you're more confident or effective at some of these, and less so at others. A blanket statement that you're "bad at your job" denies you a fair appraisal of your abilities, and will also harm your mental well-being in the process.

Limiting beliefs are also too easy on you, because they allow you to essentially give up and take a path that requires less mental effort, rather than focusing on what is actually going wrong with your circumstances. Limiting beliefs are not a virtuous way of thinking and are an antithesis to Stoicism, which asks you to take responsibility for your actions, reflect on your experiences and behavior with radical self-honesty, and, in the process, identify spaces for personal improvement.

The difference in mindsets above has been framed as the difference between a "growth mindset" and a "fixed mindset." Catherine Cote (2022) from the Harvard Business School explained the difference as follows: "Someone with a growth mindset views intelligence, abilities, and talents as learnable and capable of improvement through effort. On the other hand, someone with a fixed mindset views those same traits as inherently stable and unchangeable over time."

Limiting beliefs are a representation of a fixed mindset. On the other hand, Stoics believe that every challenge a person faces is an opportunity for personal growth, and as such are a manifestation of a growth mindset.

With Robert, the situation at his workplace caused him to initially hold several limiting beliefs:

I have no control over the situation. Robert believed that the changes in senior management, the restructuring of the team, and the additional layer of reporting were entirely beyond his control. This belief, while based in truth, led to a sense of helplessness and hindered a proactive approach to decision-making.

My manager's behavior defines my worth. Robert believed that his manager taking credit for his work and avoiding controversial discussions reflected directly on his own worth and competence. Indirectly, he believed that his manager's acknowledgment was crucial for job satisfaction. He developed a limiting belief that his value within the organization was solely determined by external validation by the likes of his seniors in the hierarchy—i.e., factors that were outside his control.

There are no opportunities for advancement. Robert felt stuck in his position with little hope of promotion. He held a limiting belief that opportunities for advancement within the organization were scarce or unavailable to him. This belief contributed to a sense of personal and career stagnation.

I cannot influence organizational change. Robert perceived the organizational culture as unchangeable and resistant to improvement and, as such, he adopted a limiting belief that his efforts to influence positive change were futile. This belief led to a lack of initiative in advocating for a better work environment.

I'm powerless in the face of office politics. Robert held the limiting belief that navigating office politics was beyond his capability and that he lacked the skills to effectively manage such dynamics. This belief contributed to a sense of disempowerment within the workplace.

I am defined by current circumstances. Robert held a limiting belief that his current position and the challenges that came with it defined his professional identity. This belief contributed to a sense of resignation to his situation, and hindered his ability to envision alternative paths out of his troubles.

My workplace is inherently unsupportive. Robert saw his workplace as inherently unsupportive and unsympathetic to his concerns. Due to this, he developed a limiting belief that seeking support or positive change to his circumstances within the organization was unrealistic.

You might have noticed that many of the above beliefs are centered around external factors: the manager's behavior, the structure of the organization, the atmosphere of the workplace, and so on. External factors like these are important, but they were not within Robert's control, and will likely not be within yours under similar circumstances. Worrying about them, or trying to exert control where you cannot, is a distraction to be resisted. Instead, Stoicism asks you to focus on what you *can* control.

As part of this, it's important to look within rather than without, especially when it comes to other people within your circumstances. Focusing on external comparisons robs you of your agency, because you can't control how other people behave. As such, your comparisons should be restricted to your own past efforts. Challenge yourself to improve, fostering your development with every opportunity.

This connects to the idea that Seneca expressed as follows: "Misfortune is virtue's opportunity" (Seneca, c.65/2018). In essence, approach each difficulty in your path with a virtuous mindset: one that exhibits courage, wisdom, moderation, and justice. And to do so, one of the first steps is to challenge the limiting beliefs that you might have.

Questions to Challenge Limiting Beliefs

A gem cannot be polished without friction, nor a man perfected without trials. – Seneca

The Stoics were profoundly optimistic about human nature. Stoicism reflects this positive view of human nature by advocating personal development whenever it is available. If you find yourself holding limiting beliefs, ask yourself the following questions to help you shift your perspective into a growth mindset:

- What is within my control?

- Am I viewing challenges as opportunities for growth?

- Is my perception of the situation objective?

- What assumptions am I making, and how valid are they?

- Am I practicing acceptance of the present moment?

- Am I overly concerned with external opinions and recognition?

- Have I cultivated an inner fortress of tranquility?

- What is the worst that can happen, and can I endure it?

- Have I considered the impermanence of the situation?

- What is the next best step to take?

- Is there anything I have overlooked?

- Can I see any obvious blind spots?

- Is there someone I should ideally talk to?

- Where can I get a fuller, more comprehensive picture of the situation?

- What else can I do to solve the problem at hand?

Robert was not viewing the challenges presented by the shift in company structure and the relationship with his manager as opportunities for growth. This was unconsciously supported by his belief that he was "stuck" in place and unable to progress from his current position within the firm. He was also overly concerned with external opinions and recognition, particularly those of his new manager and the senior executives at the firm. During the meeting where others found fault with his team, his thoughts were too focused on how management perceived his work.

Finally, Robert had not considered the impermanence of the situation, even though it had come about as the result of several changes in itself.

He had resigned himself to the whims of the organization, convincing himself that any further changes to his circumstances were beyond his means. Once he had identified his answers to the above questions, Robert was mentally prepared for the next steps toward embracing and adopting a Stoic mindset.

Developing a Stoic Mindset in the Workplace

Freedom is the only worthy goal in life. It is won by disregarding things that lie beyond our control. —Epictetus

The Stoic mindset is one of radical self-honesty. It's about learning from your past experiences with objectivity and recognizing further opportunities for more virtuous behavior. It's also about keeping a sense of perspective, and using that sense of perspective to help reduce stress in the moment.

When Robert prioritized core virtues to guide his actions, and analyzed the steps forward he could take that aligned with those virtues, this helped him find meaning and fulfillment within himself, and gradually diminished his earlier reliance on external validation. Robert also dealt with his feelings of helplessness by actively identifying factors he could control in his circumstances, and practiced a mindset of acceptance and resilience toward the factors he couldn't.

In addition, Robert mentally prepared himself for setbacks by contemplating them in advance, and simultaneously trained himself to view those challenges as opportunities; as a result, this increased the positivity in his attitude toward his situation. He reminded himself that he still had a job, unlike his friend Paul, who had been recently let go without even a severance package. Despite not being entirely at peace with his situation, Robert realized that he was still better off than many others, which was an additional contributor to the positivity he was working toward.

To resolve the issues he faced with his manager, Robert first reframed the limiting beliefs he had about those issues; he was then able to view their troubled relationship as one that was lacking in open communication, thereby creating room for improvement. To that end, Robert worked on his soft skills in order to better express himself, as well as on his assertiveness. He relied on the guidance and support of colleagues and friends to help him through this.

Robert also instilled a sense of control and purpose within himself by hashing out concrete action plans to address his work issues. He then broke down his plans into smaller, manageable tasks to give himself a better sense of progress.

As he carried out all these preparatory steps in the development of his Stoic mindset, Robert also employed mindfulness techniques such as meditation and deep breathing. These were invaluable in helping him to manage his stress, stay present, and develop emotional resilience in the face of his circumstances.

Cultivating a Stoic Mindset

The following exercises are derived not just from the principles of Stoicism, but also from CBT. They are most effective when practiced on a daily basis, as this means they can be more effectively deployed during more challenging times.

As a first and foundational step, behave with resilience, wisdom, and courage, regardless of external circumstances, when deciding on the next course of action to take. Identify the "dichotomy of control": which aspects of a situation you can control (e.g., your reactions or your work ethic) and which you cannot (e.g., *adiaphora* or "indifferent things," like decisions made by senior management). Focus your actions on the former.

"Premeditatio Malorum" (Preparation for Adversity)

Anticipate potential challenges in advance. This mentally prepares you for setbacks, thus fostering a mindset of acceptance and resilience when facing difficulties. As Seneca (c.65/2018) once said, "Something already anticipated comes as less of a shock."

Viewing Challenges as Opportunities

View workplace challenges as opportunities for professional growth, and potentially for personal improvement as well. This empowers you to approach difficulties with a positive attitude.

Cognitive Restructuring

Challenge limiting beliefs that you may have regarding your workplace difficulties. One way to do this is to to try and see the situation from different perspectives (the other person's perspective, a best friend's perspective, an HR perspective), and reframe the negative thoughts in a more balanced and constructive manner.

Realistic Goals and Problem-Solving Strategies

Set realistic and achievable goals within your current work environment. Break down larger objectives into smaller, manageable tasks to better foster a sense of accomplishment. Create concrete action plans to address these challenges.

Communication Skills and Assertiveness Training

Improve your soft skills to help navigate difficult conversations. This involves being able to express needs, set boundaries, and seek support from others when necessary. Connect with colleagues, mentors, or friends who can provide guidance, empathy, and perspective.

Practicing Mindfulness and Tranquility

Stoicism encourages the cultivation of inner tranquility and peace of mind through mindfulness techniques such as meditation, deep breathing, and progressive muscle relaxation (PMR). This helps keep your thoughts focused on the present, manage stress, and maintain emotional composure irrespective of the context.

Robert: Embracing Challenges

In the crucible of pressure, a Stoic soul emerges refined, resilient, and unshaken, for it is not the weight that breaks us but the manner in which we carry it. –
Unknown

When Robert approached his work challenges with the above mindset, he recognized that it was not external pressures but his internal responses and resilience that would determine his ability to endure those tough times, and even thrive in them. After careful reflection on his situation, and having considered various options, he decided to take a proactive approach to address the challenges he was facing in the workplace.

Robert first clarified and revisited his personal and professional values, as well as his long-term goals. This self-reflection provided Robert with a clearer understanding of whether his situation aligned with his own aspirations. He also realized that in order to move forward, he needed to express his concerns, seek feedback, and explore potential solutions with the individuals whom he had been struggling to work with before.

Before committing to any major courses of action, Robert first sought advice from his organization's HR department as well as legal counsel to better understand his rights in his circumstances, which helped him to more thoroughly explore potential remedies.

Having duly recognized that the current organizational dynamics were not aligning with his professional growth and personal well-being, Robert took the plunge and initiated an open and honest conversation with his current manager. He candidly expressed his concerns about the recent changes in the team structure, the impact on standards and motivation, and the challenges he faced in his role. The goal here was to bring about a better understanding of expectations and mutual support.

During the discussion, Robert presented a well-documented record of his contributions and achievements within the team, emphasizing the positive outcomes that had resulted from his leadership. This documentation proved to be invaluable when emphasizing the impact of his role and responsibilities. He also took the opportunity to discuss potential adjustments to his current work situation that could better align with the skills and interests he had demonstrated.

Robert also articulated his commitment to the company's success and his desire to continue contributing meaningfully. To that end, he identified areas for professional development that aligned with both his personal interests and the needs of the organization. If he acquired new skills in the process, this would make him a more valuable asset to the company, as well as a more competitive one within the industry as a whole.

Simultaneously, Robert reached out to his professional network within the organization and extended his network outside of it as well, seeking guidance and support from mentors and colleagues. He explored potential internal opportunities that might better align with his skills, interests, and career aspirations; he found the internal mobility that the available opportunities provided an effective way to get unstuck from his own situation.

While engaging in these internal efforts, Robert also began discreetly exploring external job opportunities, keeping his options open for a potential career move. He conducted this external exploration with a focus on finding a work environment that valued his expertise and provided a better cultural fit. This proactive approach turned out to provide Robert with many potential alternative paths for career advancement, as well as inspiration for his current work. He even took some time to consider entrepreneurial opportunities that leveraged his skills and passions. Some of the possibilities he explored included starting a side project or business that aligned with his expertise.

Throughout all this activity, Robert focused on developing emotional resilience via mindfulness, stress management techniques, and support systems. This helped Robert navigate all his challenges with a clearer mind.

By taking this multifaceted approach, Robert overcame his struggles with a combination of open communication, internal exploration, and external opportunities. This decision reflected his commitment to proactively managing his career, focusing on what was within his control while staying true to his Stoic principles.

Chapter 2:

Self-Reflection and Meditation

It is not that we have a short time to live, but that we waste much of it. –Seneca

When facing a personal setback, it is natural to dwell on the disappointment that comes with the setback. Stoicism advocates for making use of that time and mental energy more productively, to focus on lessons learned and future growth rather than the misfortune brought about by trying times. Marion took this advice to heart when she faced some particularly trying circumstances of her own.

Marion was a seasoned professional in marketing when she faced a significant career challenge that tested her resilience and professional identity. Having dedicated over a decade to her role, Marion found herself in a leadership position after her boss's departure, entrusted with the responsibilities of the entire local team.

For nearly a year, Marion shouldered the additional burden of her boss's responsibilities while carrying out her own role. This period coincided with the absence of the department head due to illness, creating a vacuum in leadership within the team. Despite the challenges, Marion diligently managed the responsibilities, ensuring the team's continued success.

While Marion's dedicated efforts kept her team afloat, new managers were appointed within the department to address the departures of the various lead personnel. Unfortunately, these individuals were unfamiliar with Marion's long-standing contributions and did not fully appreciate the depth of her role. The dynamics began to shift as the head of the department remained absent during this crucial period.

The vacancy in her boss's position, left open due to the department head's prolonged absence, became a pivotal moment in Marion's career. The leadership role was advertised internally and externally. To

Marion's surprise, considering she was effectively undertaking the same responsibilities herself at the time, she wasn't encouraged to apply for the position. Still, she decided to pursue the opportunity against the odds.

So Marion applied for the position, driven by her years of experience, her dedication, and the contributions she had already made to the team's success. Despite hearing rumors of other team leaders being considered for the role, Marion secured an interview. The interview process became a crucial juncture in her professional journey.

Unfortunately, Marion did not secure the coveted leadership position. The disappointment weighed heavily on her, as she grappled with the disconnect between her perceived value and the organizational decision; she felt like she had been exploited at their convenience and then tossed aside. The experience left her questioning her standing within the company and her future trajectory.

The Power of Self-Reflection

You have power over your mind, not outside events. Realize this, and you will find strength. –Marcus Aurelius

Personal or professional setbacks are always challenging; after all, no one enjoys being disappointed and feeling used. However, Stoicism holds that in these moments of difficulty, there is opportunity for personal growth.

In the last chapter, we discussed the importance of challenging limiting beliefs that can contribute to a fixed mindset. As part of this, it is important to engage in honest self-reflection, which requires a great deal of practical wisdom. This wisdom is one of the four Stoic virtues, and by wisely examining our own experiences and behaviors, we can identify areas for growth. As Seneca (c.65/2018) wrote: "This is what makes us evil—that none of us looks back upon our own lives. We reflect upon only that which we are about to do. And yet our plans for the future descend from the past."

Drawing on the above Stoic philosophy, Marion reflected on the aspects within and outside of her control (the dichotomy of control). During this initial self-reflection, she embraced Stoic virtues that emphasized the importance of being principled in her professional conduct despite external challenges. She acknowledged that the decisions of others were beyond her control and chose to focus instead on her own growth and development. As such, Marion adapted to the changing dynamics, recognizing that her leadership journey might take a different course than initially anticipated.

Stoicism is about personal responsibility, which means that it is also about recognizing that we can always control our response to external events, even if we cannot control those events themselves. It is about focusing on our own thoughts and behaviors without ceding power to the external events that act on us or around us. In this way, Stoicism is empowering. However, it also means that we have to take responsibility.

One day, when Marian was walking alone in the woods for exercise, she realized that she had allowed herself to take on the extra responsibilities for a year without clarifying and integrating them into her job description. It had been her previous manager who had unofficially distributed the workload to her. Marion realized that since her old manager had left, she had grown to dislike key members of the new management team, and that this could explain her present noncommittal attitude toward the role.

Epictetus (c.108/2008) said that "No man is free who is not master of himself." And the first step to mastering our own thoughts and behaviors is to understand what makes us tick. Wisdom demands that we understand our own nature and honestly identify our strengths and weaknesses going forward.

Proper self-reflection is powerful because it is comprised of two components: ethical self-reflection, in which we are encouraged to be a better person in adherence to Stoic principles, and cognitive self-reflection, in which we come up with actionable plans to make that change happen. To make the best use of this practice, aim to approach self-reflection like a scientist: with curiosity and objectivity.

Albert Ellis, the father of CBT, explicitly noted that his theories were inspired by Stoicism (Digiuseppe et al., 2013). At the core of CBT is the *cognitive cycle,* a representation of how our behaviors, thoughts, feelings, and physical sensations are causally interrelated in all directions. Our behaviors affect our thoughts, our physical sensations affect our feelings, our feelings affect our behaviors, and so on—and vice versa. As a rudimentary example, if we are angry (a feeling), this may cause our pulse rate to quicken (a physical sensation).

Because behaviors, thoughts, feelings, and physical sensations all have causal influence over each other, we can focus on those aspects that are more tractable. It's hard—maybe impossible—to change feelings directly. However, we can challenge limiting beliefs or abstain from unproductive behavioral patterns. And through the cognitive cycle, it follows that changing our thought patterns and behavior can have a positive influence on how we feel.

These insights from CBT can be used in cognitive self-reflection. By being aware of the cognitive cycle, we can identify triggers and patterns, giving us better opportunities for positive change. Reflect on a recent challenge, and think back: How you were feeling? What physical sensations were you experiencing? What behaviors were you exhibiting? Lastly, what thoughts were you thinking?

Marion was able to move forward and face the crossroads of her career after drawing emotional resilience and strength from Stoic principles. After self-reflecting, she contemplated her next steps, aiming to cultivate an inner fortitude that would guide her through future challenges, and knowing that her journey was shaped by her responses to adversity rather than the adversity itself.

Reflecting on Challenges

Our life is what our thoughts make it. –Marcus Aurelius

When reflecting on and working through the disappointment and other negative feelings Marion felt after the rejection of her application, she asked herself a series of questions inspired by the perspectives of both Stoic philosophy and CBT. By looking at these questions in more detail, we can get an idea of what to focus on during the kind of deep, thorough, and honest self-reflection that Stoicism encourages:

What aspects of this situation are beyond my control? How can I practice acceptance of these elements and focus on what I can influence? What factors within my control can I focus on that will improve my current situation?

In Marion's situation, an external candidate with international experience had already been identified for the position before the interview process. This had taken place independently of her own work; her actions had neither contributed to nor worked directly against this particular event.

How can I reframe the narrative of this experience to emphasize the opportunities for personal and professional growth, regardless of the outcome?

When Marion eventually overcame the initial disappointment of being rejected, she realized that it was her ego that had been hurt more than anything else. She took a look at her own resume and accomplishments, with an eye for where it could be improved so that a future rejection would be less likely.

How can I develop a mindset of embracing my future, even if it deviates from my initial expectations? How can I align these changed circumstances with my ambitions going forward? How might this setback contribute to my overall journey? Can I still feel joy in the present moment, despite feeling deprived of the promotion?

What automatic thoughts come to mind when I think about the setback I am facing? Are there recurring negative thought patterns?

Marion was able to identify some deep-seated feelings of resentment she had toward her manager when she contemplated the above.

Do I engage in cognitive distortions when reflecting on this situation, such as catastrophizing or overgeneralization? How can I challenge and reframe these distortions?

How can I objectively assess the evidence for and against my thoughts about not securing the position? If I were in HR, how would I view the strength of my application versus that of the chosen candidate? What alternative, more balanced thoughts can I cultivate?

How can I stay engaged in activities that bring fulfillment and a sense of accomplishment? What coping strategies resonate with me to navigate the emotional impact of this setback? How can I incorporate these strategies into my daily routine?

These actions need not be directly related to the source of the setback. For instance, Marion organized a night out with her friends to boost her morale.

What practical steps can I take to address the challenges that contributed to me not achieving a desirable outcome? How can I develop a plan for future career aspirations?

When Marion approached HR requesting more feedback, HR explained to her that the business manager needed a candidate with very specific qualifications, including at least five years of managerial experience in an international environment. Having heard this, Marion better understood the business need, and felt less resentful toward her employer and more at peace with herself. She also discussed with HR how she could upskill for a potential mid-managerial position.

After the conversation with HR, Marion set about researching courses to improve her CV. She had also been having discussions with her husband at home about starting a family; it seemed poignantly ideal to both start a family and begin upskilling at the same time. Marion chose do an editing course, as this would enhance her CV on the one hand while also enabling her to work as a freelance editor and potentially create her own online business while on maternity leave. Marion felt happy and empowered by the potential of this next step; she managed to reframe her professional disappointment into an opportunity and the beginning of a new chapter of her life from both a personal and professional perspective.

By engaging in these reflective questions from both a Stoic and a CBT perspective, Marion was able to gain valuable insights into her thought processes, emotional responses, and actionable steps to navigate the disappointment of her leadership setback constructively. The same applies to you: Balancing Stoic acceptance with practical CBT tools can provide a comprehensive framework for your own self-reflection and growth.

Incorporating Meditation Into Your Daily Routine

Happy is the man who has broken the chains which hurt the mind, and has given up worrying once and for all. –Ovid

Self-reflection is not always easy. You need to be firm and honest with yourself, but this is only half of the difficulty. Be perceptive and self-aware as well, so you can identify the physical sensations you're feeling, the thoughts you're having, and the emotions you're experiencing. Consequently, it is useful to engage in meditative and mindfulness techniques. These improve your awareness of the present so you can engage in more effective self-reflection later.

Incorporating meditation into your daily routine isn't very time-consuming and benefits you in many ways. Daily meditation improves the quality of your self-reflection, helps you regulate your emotions and reduce stress, boosts your well-being, and improves your general efficiency.

With this in mind, here's a simple guided mindful meditation that anyone seeking to enhance their well-being can incorporate into their daily life:

1. Sit in a comfortable position, on either a chair or a cushion. Ensure your back is straight, your hands are resting in your lap, and your feet are flat on the ground. Close your eyes gently. Take a few deep breaths, inhaling through your nose and exhaling through your mouth. Allow each breath to anchor you in the present moment.

2. Start at the top of your head and gradually move your awareness down your body. Notice any areas of tension or

discomfort, and try to release any tightness with each breath, allowing your body to relax. Shift your attention to your breath. Notice the sensation of each inhale and exhale. Feel the rise and fall of your chest or the coolness of the breath as it enters your nostrils.

3. As thoughts arise, acknowledge them without judgment. Imagine each thought as a passing cloud in the sky. Let them come and go, returning your focus to your breathing. Bring to mind something you're grateful for. It could be a person, an experience, or even the present moment. Allow a sense of gratitude to fill your heart. Integrate Stoic principles by reflecting on what is within your control and what is not. Embrace acceptance of external circumstances, finding strength in your responses.

4. Repeat a positive affirmation or mantra silently. Choose words that resonate with your goals and aspirations, fostering a positive mindset, like the following: *I embrace the present moment with gratitude, accepting what is within my control and letting go of what is not. With each breath, I cultivate resilience and inner strength, knowing that challenges are opportunities for growth. I am grounded in the present, and I trust in my ability to navigate life's twists with grace and wisdom. I have opened my mind to new ideas and perspectives on my situation, so I can confidently move forward from it.*

5. Gradually bring your awareness back to the room. Gently open your eyes. Take a moment to acknowledge the tranquility you've cultivated. As you go about your day, carry the sense of mindfulness with you. When faced with challenges, return to your breath and the principles of resilience you've cultivated.

When Marion incorporated this mindful meditation into her daily routine, it provided her with a valuable space for self-reflection, emotional regulation, and the cultivation of a Stoic mindset. Regular practice enhances resilience and the capacity to overcome professional and personal struggles with grace and inner strength.

More Techniques for Mindful Introspection

4–7–8 Breathing

This brief yet highly effective breathing exercise can help reduce stress in the moment and ground you in your awareness of the present. First, inhale through your nose for four seconds. Then, hold the breath for seven seconds. Next, exhale through your mouth for eight seconds (the name of the technique comes from these time periods). Repeat the same cycle of inhaling, holding your breath, and exhaling another three times, or until you feel more grounded.

Cognitive and Ethical Self-Reflection

Cognitive self-reflection focuses on the more logical, factual, and action-oriented aspects of the events you want to reflect upon. You can also think of it as self-reflection that engages the left side or hemisphere of the brain.

First, choose an event from your day that you want to reflect on. Then lay out the facts: what happened, where and when it happened, and who was there. Write these facts down in your journal or on a piece of paper. Identify the following, writing down your answers:

- **The physical sensations you were feeling:** Were you feeling hungry, tired, tense, or hot?

- **The emotions you were experiencing:** Were you feeling irritable, angry, or stressed?

- **The thoughts you were having:** Did they have a theme, or do they remind you of anyone else in your life?

- **How you behaved:** Were you clenching your jaw or tensing your shoulders?

Next, reflect on how your physical sensations, emotions, thoughts, and behaviors might have influenced each other. Take the time to understand how these aspects interlinked, and why the event unfolded as it did. Finally, think about simple interventions you might have made, especially in terms of managing your physical sensations, thoughts, and behaviors. This will provide action plans for the future.

In contrast to the above, *ethical self-reflection* focuses on the more emotional, perceptual, and attitude-oriented aspects of the events you want to reflect upon. It can also be considered as self-reflection that engages the right side or hemisphere of the brain.

As a first step, choose an event from your day that you want to reflect on. Then, again lay out the basic facts: what happened, where and when it happened, and who was there. Write these facts down in your journal or on a piece of paper. In addition, write down how you reacted to the event. You can incorporate elements of cognitive self-reflection here if you like. Next, consider how an impeccable person might have ideally behaved in the same circumstances. Lastly, think about how you might get closer to that ideal in similar events in the future.

It's important not to fall into the temptation of beating yourself up. The ideally impeccable person is, after all, *ideal*, and everyone falls short of that from time to time—even the pre-eminent Stoic practitioners like Marcus Aurelius and Seneca had their moments of failure. Instead of miring yourself in your mistakes, gently identify ways in which you could have been more principled, and commit to making efforts in that direction in the future.

Marion: Gaining a Fresh Perspective

In the crucible of setback, a Stoic leader forges not in the fire of failure but in the wisdom to reshape challenges into stepping stones toward growth. —Unknown

Marion eventually viewed her setback not as a failure but as an opportunity for transformation. She recognized the importance of cultivating resilience in the face of setbacks. Instead of succumbing to disappointment, she committed herself to building inner strength and adaptability. Understanding that continuous learning and growth were still within her control, she decided to invest in her professional development. She identified areas for improvement and sought opportunities to enhance her skills.

Marion acknowledged the value of networking and relationships in the workplace. She proactively engaged in networking events, fostering connections with colleagues and leaders who appreciated her contributions. During this process, seeking mentorship became a priority for Marion. She reached out to experienced professionals within and outside the organization, gaining valuable insights and guidance for her career journey.

Marion reframed her career goals, recognizing that the setback was not a permanent roadblock but a redirection. She also set new, realistic goals that aligned with her evolving aspirations and the skills she aimed to develop.

Embracing Stoic principles, Marion shifted her mindset toward focusing on what she could control. She relinquished attachment to external outcomes and embraced the journey, valuing the process as much as the destination. Marion remained open to unforeseen opportunities, and even embraced them. Rather than fixating on a specific career path, she looked for purpose and fulfillment in the present moment and whatever opportunities unfolded.

Marion's decision to approach the situation with a combination of Stoic resilience and practical strategies from CBT allowed her to navigate the disappointment constructively. While the leadership position may not have materialized as expected, Marion found a renewed sense of purpose and direction on her professional journey.

Chapter 3:

Resilience in the Face of Adversity

He who has a why to live can bear almost any how. –Friedrich Nietzsche (In M. K., 2023)

Personal crises come in many forms, from the termination of a job to the passing away of a close family member. What they all have in common is how incredibly painful and depleting they can be to experience. In such times, it can help to draw strength from meditating on the above quote; it speaks to finding purpose and meaning in the face of even the most challenging of circumstances.

Oliver found himself unexpectedly facing a deeply troubling situation after being married for a decade. He acknowledged that he hadn't always been the perfect husband, and would admit that he regularly manipulated and played mind games with his wife; even so, the rapid deterioration of his marriage took him by surprise. The difficulty reached a peak when, following his wife Regina's diagnosis of a serious illness, she made the painful decision to leave him and take their children with her. This marked an unimaginably tough period for Oliver, who found himself grappling with a profound sense of loss and bewilderment.

The impact of this life-altering event was made worse by his wife's accusations: She claimed that Oliver had sabotaged their relationship by gaslighting her, repeatedly making false allegations against her, denying the reality that she lived in, and stonewalling her. She concluded that he was a destructive force in the family unit, and went so far as to accuse him of contributing to the onset of her illness. The weight of these claims left Oliver feeling not only abandoned but also burdened with guilt and confusion. The shattered family dynamic became a source of profound sorrow for him, with the partial separation from his children adding an extra layer of emotional complexity to an already challenging situation.

Oliver, grappling with the turmoil of his feelings and a sense of disorientation, found himself at a crossroads. The pain and confusion of this unforeseen adversity left him uncertain about the next steps in his life. He was confronted with the daunting task of not only rebuilding his personal identity but also envisioning a future that had been drastically altered by circumstances beyond his control, even if he might have been indirectly responsible for some of them. It was then that he turned to Stoicism for help.

Seeking Answers From Within

Fate leads the willing, and drags along the reluctant. –Seneca

An honest and comprehensive self-reflection is a great help when facing challenging circumstances. However, Oliver's troubles were of a more personal nature, and therefore his emotions were understandably more entangled in his woes. As such, Oliver's self-reflection needed to be geared toward building his emotional resilience.

Oliver began by looking back at his past through an objective and Stoic lens as well as he could manage, given his emotional turmoil. He reflected upon the following questions:

What was my role in the relationship dynamics? Oliver reflected on his actions and his contributions to his marriage with Regina. He acknowledged both his strengths and areas for improvement, such as his punctuality and reliability when attending important events of hers (for the former) and his tendency to manipulate and play mind games with Regina (for the latter).

What were the warning signs that I missed? Oliver reflected on whether there were subtle signs or signals in the relationship that may have indicated strain or dissatisfaction and, if so, why they went unnoticed. He then realized he had started to take Regina's presence in his life for granted, and in the process he had regressed to the emotionally distant man he had been before falling in love with Regina for the first time.

Did I communicate and set expectations effectively? Oliver reflected on his communication style and effectiveness. This led to the realization that the last few years of communication between them had been mainly arguments and disagreements. He then examined his expectations of the relationship, his spouse Regina, and himself, and assessed whether these expectations were realistic. He recalled that he would frequently tell her she was lucky to have him, which was an unbalanced and self-centered expectation in hindsight.

Did I seek feedback or critically analyze my relationship? Oliver thought about whether he actively sought feedback from Regina about the relationship, any concerns, or areas for improvement. He reflected on his openness to constructive criticism. In doing so, he saw that he had been too eager to focus on his professional growth to question the status quo of his relationship.

Were there unresolved issues or blind spots in my view of the relationship? Oliver considered whether there were unresolved issues in the relationship that might have contributed to the separation. He realized he had exhibited a tendency to either pass the buck or bury his head in the sand during the hard times. He realized, with an understandable amount of guilt, that he had been unsupportive and even dismissive of Regina when she had first pointed out the early symptoms of her illness to him.

After thoroughly analyzing the events that led up to his turmoil, including the part that he had played in those events, Oliver then looked toward the future for the next stage of his self-reflection. In particular, after consolidating all his various reflections, he began by employing the Stoic principle of dichotomy of control: He tried to focus on what he could still control, in order to get to grips with his situation. Oliver also relied on the CBT techniques of challenging his negative thoughts and practicing self-compassion. In his state of shock, he needed both of these to come to terms with the breakup and his past mistakes without spiraling into a flurry of self-imposed attacks on his self-worth. As it so happens, these are also some of the crucial first steps toward developing emotional resilience, particularly in the face of adversity.

Building Emotional Resilience

Difficulties strengthen the mind, as labor does the body. –Seneca

Emotional resilience is far broader than how we respond to a disaster, and this is why Stoicism asks us to foster it on a day-to-day basis. By strengthening our resilience, we will be able to overcome a range of emotional stresses without too much difficulty. It is important to note, though, that emotional resilience is *not* the same as being emotionless. In spite of the modern connotations of the word "stoic"—a word that has come to mean someone who can endure hardships without displaying any feelings—the Stoics in fact advocated for a healthy expression of emotions and embraced what they referred to as "emotional awareness."

What emotional resilience entails, instead, is the ability to allow ourselves to feel emotions without sacrificing our mental fortitude or the rest of our capabilities as a rational person in the process. It involves being able to detach from our emotions as we feel them and focus on controllable factors, actionable steps, achievable goals, and an overarching perspective of a situation.

This can sound like a formidable feat to accomplish at first glance, but it is far more achievable than it sounds. The following are a series of daily exercises inspired by Stoicism that help build and foster emotional resilience. These can be practiced at any stage of life—it is not necessary to begin them when facing an emotional crisis, like Oliver did. No matter the starting point, though, they are still effective as long as they are followed regularly.

Journaling and Emotional Awareness

Maintain a journal to document your thoughts and emotions; writing can provide clarity and serve as an outlet for processing feelings. Use the exercise to allow yourself to acknowledge and express the range of emotions you are experiencing—whether it's sadness, anger, confusion, or a mix of emotions.

Oliver initially used his journal to release all his pent-up emotions about the split from Regina. He could see when he read through his journal afterward that he was mentally persecuting Regina and blaming her for his misfortunes, while at the same time absolving himself of all wrongdoing by perceiving himself as a victim. A part of him knew this to be unfair, but he nevertheless couldn't stop himself from deliberately making disparaging remarks about her in front of everyone and anyone who was prepared to listen, as this sense of personal vengeance temporarily numbed his own pain. When he took the time to reflect on this, he knew he had to change his mindset.

Focusing on the Controllable and Setting Realistic Goals

Differentiate between what you can and cannot control, and direct your energy and efforts toward the latter. Establish realistic goals within your sphere of influence for emotional well-being, personal growth, and rebuilding aspects of your life where needed. Break down long-term goals into manageable steps.

As Oliver found it difficult to immediately shift the blame away from Regina, he decided to focus on the Stoic principle of "virtue in adversity." As Seneca (c.65/2018) said, "God sets us back not to punish us but to give us an opportunity to do something courageous and thereby increase our chances of attaining the highest possible excellence," "A man needs to be put to the test if he is to gain self-knowledge," and "Only by trying does he learn what his capacities are." As a goal, Oliver promised himself that this would be the best year of his life. This pact with himself gave him the courage to pick himself up and turn his life around.

Challenging Negativity and Affirming Positivity

Actively challenge negative thoughts or limiting beliefs about current circumstances. Replace irrational thoughts with more balanced and realistic perspectives. Incorporate positive affirmations into this process to help counteract any further negativity. Celebrate any recent victories, no matter how small, and channel that positivity toward your affirmations. Use mindfulness apps or similar guidance to support emotional well-being. Avoid negative coping strategies that might provide short-term relief but are detrimental in the long run.

Practicing Gratitude

Practicing gratitude can build your emotional resilience because it can put into perspective those minor complaints and stressors that would otherwise send you into a spin. It reminds us to appreciate the fact that the good far outweighs the bad, allowing us to tolerate irritating external events with a calmer countenance.

Cultivate a habit of gratitude by regularly reflecting on all the positive aspects of your life, no matter how small or insignificant. This can be incorporated into both your journaling and your positive affirmation practices.

Self-Compassion and Forgiveness

Treat yourself with kindness and understanding during this moment of difficulty. Practice self-compassion by acknowledging your imperfections and past mistakes without self-criticism. Cultivate forgiveness, not necessarily for others, but for personal growth. Release the burden of holding onto resentment or anger.

Oliver overcame a significant milestone in his own healing story when he finally consciously decided to redirect his insatiable appetite to still try and control Regina, and to regularly lash out at her in an effort to hurt and punish her, into a constructive and purposeful project. He knew that if he didn't do this, he would repeat the same pattern of hurting, blaming, and punishing the women closest to him instead of simply setting aside his pride and ego and facing up to his own issues. This allowed him to move on from his past regrets and work to improve his future self.

Prioritizing Self-Care

Work toward a physically healthy lifestyle by way of balanced nutrition, regular exercise, and sufficient sleep. Engage in activities that promote relaxation and mindfulness, such as taking walks, practicing yoga, meditating, or performing deep breathing exercises, to manage stress and stay present. Define and set personal emotional boundaries to protect your well-being. Recognize when to set limits in relationships for the sake of your self-care.

At first, Oliver didn't have time to engage in any self-care practices while he grappled with the emptiness of his own circumstances and the tension surrounding his upcoming divorce case. But thanks to his focus on Stoicism, and with the help of some friends, he was able to engage in some relaxing activities and allow himself a chance to recuperate.

Maintaining a Social Support System

Share experiences and feelings with a trusted support network. Work to stay in touch in even the smallest of ways. Engage in social activities to foster a sense of belonging and connection. Consider engaging with a therapist or counselor to explore your emotions, gain insights, and develop coping strategies. Likewise, connect with support groups where individuals share similar experiences. Shared narratives can foster a sense of community and understanding.

Rediscovering Passions, Hobbies, and Interests

Rediscover or explore new hobbies and interests that bring joy and fulfillment. Engage in activities outside the sphere of the source of your adversarial circumstances to renew your sense of purpose. This can also be a chance to explore new opportunities, whether they be in career development or personal interests. Learn to embrace change as a chance for renewal and growth.

Establishing a Routine and Cultivating Adaptability

Create a daily routine around your non-Stoic activities as well, in order to provide structure and predictability to your life and potentially contribute to a sense of stability during turbulent times. At the same time, recognize that life is dynamic and subject to change, and work on skills to navigate uncertainties with flexibility and adaptability.

Building resilience is a continuous process that involves commitment and self-compassion. Oliver was encouraged to approach these steps at his own pace and to seek support when needed. Over time, these strategies helped contribute to his ability to cope with adversity and cultivate resilience.

Cultivating Inner Strength

He is a wise man who does not grieve for the things which he has not, but rejoices for those which he has. –Epictetus

Inner strength, or mental fortitude, is a quality that goes hand-in-hand with emotional resilience. A Stoic principle that readily favors inner strength is that of *premeditatio malorum*, or "preparation for adversity." This is the principle that asks us to contemplate potential challenges we might face in future so we can mentally prepare to respond to them should they arise.

One method of taking this principle a step further is to actively engage in situations on a smaller scale, or with less drastic consequences, that evoke the same challenges. For instance, the child custody case was still pending. In the meantime, Olivier focused on getting an apartment with an extra bedroom for his kids. He also focused on providing as stable an environment as possible for his kids ahead of the custody judgment.

The following are further practices that can lead to improved inner strength:

Developing Assertiveness, Courage, and Empathy

Oliver recognized that in the past, in an effort to avoid problems, he had inadvertently incited conflict by simply ignoring or denying issues. Going forward, he decided that instead of avoiding issues, he would avoid cowardice, hesitation, and dread in facing future challenging situations, striving to be his best self in every situation. In this way, he worked on developing his courage.

Like Oliver, identify and confront your own fears or anxieties in a gradual manner. Embrace courage as a willingness to step outside your comfort zones. Develop assertiveness in expressing your needs and boundaries. Stand up for yourself more, and learn to communicate effectively in challenging situations—perhaps from attending workshops or interacting with people from your support network.

Following the above, enhance communication skills to express your thoughts and feelings more clearly. Develop the ability to navigate interpersonal relationships with empathy. Use this to strengthen existing relationships and cultivate new connections.

Persistence and Grit

When pursuing your goals, develop grit and determination by maintaining perseverance in the face of challenges. Setbacks are likely inevitable; view them as temporary and as opportunities for learning. Reframe them as part of the journey toward personal growth.

Humor and Lightheartedness

Cultivate a sense of humor and playfulness. Seek joy in small moments and work to maintain a lighthearted perspective. Engage in activities that bring laughter and joy, and make use of the therapeutic benefits of humor in reducing stress.

Contributions to the Community

Identify ways to contribute to the well-being of others. Find meaning in making a positive impact on individuals or the community. For example, engaging in volunteer work or helping others through community activities can provide a sense of purpose and perspective.

Oliver: Fostering Resilience

In the tempest of personal crisis, a Stoic heart weathers the storm not with resistance, but with the resilience to find solace in the depth of its own calm. –Unknown

Oliver eventually approached his personal crisis with the necessary tranquility and resilience. In challenging times, one can find strength by embracing a sense of inner calm and navigating the storm with a Stoic mindset. In the face of his adversity, Oliver realized things had to change, so he decided to seek help and realign his life with his passions and values. For instance, he loved to deal in real estate; once the sale of their house came through, he invested in a couple of period properties that qualified for state grants for renovation purposes. He planned to build a portfolio of 20 properties over time to supplement his pension; this gave him a new drive to excel at work.

Oliver sought professional guidance from a therapist who provided valuable insights and coping strategies. Through introspection, he cultivated self-awareness and learned to navigate his emotions with grace. Oliver also connected with a support group where he found solace in shared experiences and built meaningful connections.

Inspired by Stoic principles and a commitment to personal growth, Oliver decided to view the separation not as a failure but as an opportunity for renewal. He set realistic goals for himself, focusing on both short-term achievements and long-term aspirations. By embracing a growth mindset, Oliver discovered the resilience within him to face life's uncertainties.

In his pursuit of a more fulfilling life, Oliver rekindled old passions and explored new interests. He engaged in activities that brought him joy and purpose, forming a foundation for his journey toward healing. He also set up a profile on a couple of dating apps; he had never used them before, and was very skeptical, but was pleasantly surprised to meet some newly separated women. This gave him the impetus to start considering a new potentially romantic relationship.

Recognizing the importance of healthy communication, he initiated a candid conversation with his ex-wife Regina. They agreed to establish clear boundaries and open lines of communication, fostering a sense of closure and understanding. As time passed, Oliver's resilience and newfound perspective allowed him to rebuild his relationship with his children. Through shared moments of laughter, support, and understanding, Oliver began to forge a new chapter in his life.

Ultimately, Oliver's story became one of triumph over adversity. His decision to embrace change, prioritize self-care, and foster resilience not only transformed his own life but also inspired those around him. The narrative of Oliver's resilience serves as a testament to the human capacity for growth and renewal in the face of personal challenges.

Chapter 4:

Finding Meaning and Purpose

Waste no more time arguing about what a good man should be. Be one. —Marcus Aurelius

The journey through life is undertaken largely due to the sense of purpose and meaning that is derived from it. One of the hardest challenges to face is a loss of or drastic reduction in those qualities. An alignment with Stoic principles can help purpose and contentment to be rediscovered in a life that lacks it. Morris relied on these principles to overcome his own struggles when his life underwent a shift in focus.

Morris dedicated the entirety of his professional life to the insurance industry, demonstrating unwavering commitment and expertise. Last year, the landscape of the business shifted as new opportunities dwindled, prompting senior management to implement a voluntary redundancy plan. Morris, who had been a stalwart in the industry, found himself at a crossroads.

With a nudge from his manager, Morris opted for a voluntary redundancy package, viewing it as an early retirement opportunity. However, what followed was an unforeseen struggle that took a toll on his well-being. Six months into his retirement, Morris found himself grappling with unexpected emotions. In particular, he harbored a pervasive sense of depression and deep-seated feelings of anxiety in relation to what the future might hold.

The transition from a bustling career to the unfamiliar terrain of retirement proved more challenging than Morris had anticipated. While he initially embraced the prospect of leisure and relaxation, the reality of not having a daily job to occupy his time began to weigh heavily on him. The monotony of each day and the absence of the professional rhythm he had known for years left Morris feeling adrift.

Seeking solace and emotional support, Morris turned to his family. However, the adjustment to this new phase of life persisted as a formidable challenge. The void left by the absence of daily work responsibilities, compounded by the emotional toll of navigating retirement, led Morris into a space of unexpected despondency.

As Morris grappled with these unanticipated emotional struggles, the need for a holistic approach to retirement and well-being became evident. His journey now involved not only adapting to the practical aspects of a post-work life but also addressing the emotional and psychological facets that retirement can unveil.

In the quiet moments after Morris retired, he meditated on endings: his last day in college, the day each of his kids left home, his last day at work, the last time he saw his parents before they died. He meditated on the reality that every moment that passes will be the last time to live those moments. He thought about the future: the day he would see his wife, or the rest of his world, for the last time. Someday, there would be no tomorrow. He also imagined being in a retirement home and wishing he was at home, sitting in his armchair reading the daily newspaper like he was right now. He knew deep down that even if he had ended a big chapter of his life, there was still much to be experienced and enjoyed in life, and he decided then and there that he was determined to make the most of it.

Identifying Core Values

Know, first, who you are, and then adorn yourself accordingly. –Epictetus

The meaning that is derived from a life is often intricately tied with how the four Stoic virtues and similar concepts such as core values are perceived. In essence, we often develop meaning in our lives through the application of these virtues and values. Through the Stoic tradition of self-reflection, we can identify our core values to allow us to remain true to them even as our circumstances shift in nature.

With that said, core values can also change gradually due to time and the effects of life experiences. It is important to identify values that are significant in the present, rather than values that meant more in the past than they do now.

The following are some questions that can help identify one's core values; they have been juxtaposed with Morris's own answers to give an idea of how a set of core values could be derived from them.

What was the proudest moment of your life? Morris's proudest moment was when he was given an award in recognition of his years of service and excellence in the insurance industry. This suggested hard work and commitment as core values.

When did you feel most ashamed? Morris felt ashamed at the recollection of a time he let down a friend who had been relying on him. This suggested friendship and trust as core values, since it was the breaking of trust and betrayal of friendship that was the source of the shame.

Who do you most admire, and what do you admire about them? Morris admired Chris Gardner, the motivational businessman and stockbroker, for how he achieved monumental success from poor, homeless beginnings. This suggested resilience and persistence as core values.

When are you most happy? Morris felt happiest when he was busy engaging his mind with some kind of problem to solve or project to oversee. This suggested mental stimulation as a core value.

What do you appreciate most about yourself? Morris appreciated how he often came up with creative solutions to problems he faced during his work in insurance. This suggested creativity as a core value.

Sometimes, different answers may indicate the same core values, which remain as valid values regardless; for Morris, his admiration for Chris Gardner and his pride in his own award of recognition both pointed to hard work and persistence as core values.

Setting Meaningful Goals

A ship should not ride on a single anchor, nor life on a single hope. –Epictetus

Morris had a small stroke of fortune regarding the next step in his search for new meaning and purpose. While cleaning his house, he stumbled across a dusty journal from his youth, in which there was a list of goals he had penned down years ago—dreams that had taken a backseat amid the hustle and bustle of career and responsibilities.

Such a list of former goals to use as a basis certainly helps, but is not a necessity when it comes to setting meaningful goals. However, when combined with the core values identified from before, these former aspirations become instrumental in giving shape to a newer set of meaningful goals worth embarking upon.

Setting Goals Based on Core Values

The following are some exercises that can help guide the formation of meaningful goals, with the usage of both newly affirmed core values and a reflection on past circumstances as a basis.

Take time to reflect on the principles and values that matter most to the present you. Think about the ideals you hold dear, and how they influence your choices and actions. Assess your current life against these values. Are your daily decisions and actions in harmony with what you hold as deeply important?

Consider whether you experience nagging feelings or a lingering sense that there might be unexplored dimensions of your life or untapped potential waiting to be realized? Reflect on the ways in which your current life choices may have drifted from the values that once guided you, as well as from the Stoic virtues of courage, justice, moderation, and wisdom. Evaluate the overarching purpose of your life. Contemplate the ways in which it has become disconnected from your passions and values.

Look back on the dreams or goals you harbored in the past that got buried in the course of life's demands. Some mementos or a journal like Morris's may make this process easier. Reconsider those dreams and goals in the context of your current situation. Think about how much they still matter to you, as well as how achievable they are in the present.

Mentally envision future scenarios where you are living in alignment with your core values. Think about how this makes you feel, and identify changes as well as elements that strike you as particularly actionable. Consider activities or causes that ignite genuine passion within you, or that bring a sense of joy and fulfillment. If any of these passions are unfeasible due to your current situation, look into similar alternatives that could elicit the same feelings within you. Look for any sense of curiosity or restlessness nudging you to explore new territories, whether they be in your career, personal pursuits, or relationships.

Regularly write down your thoughts on paper to explore your notions on values, purpose, and aspirations. Write freely about what matters most to you, without editing your thoughts as you write them down.

The words on the pages of his journal may have resonated more with a younger, more aspirational version of Morris, but a spark of curiosity still ignited within him, prompting him to consider whether these early aspirations still held relevance. By responding to the reflective questions that his journal as well as his Stoic mindset prompted, Morris was encouraged to reassess his goals, reconnect with his values, and consider potential untapped reservoirs of purpose waiting to be explored.

Creating a Personal Mission Statement

If a man knows not to which port he sails, no wind is favorable. –Marcus Aurelius

The Stoics often advocated for big-picture thinking, or having a "view from above," together with a focus on controllable, actionable details. To achieve this, reframe your goals in the form of a concise summary of your search for meaning and purpose, creating a personal mission statement.

A personal mission statement serves as a guiding compass, aligning your actions with your values, fostering resilience, and ultimately nudging you toward a meaningful and fulfilling life. By integrating elements of Stoicism and CBT, the end result is a holistic approach that aligns with values, principles, and practical strategies for personal growth and renewed purpose. The following is a step-by-step guide to laying the groundwork for, and then creating, such a statement:

Step 1: Reflecting on Core Values

Begin by reflecting on how to integrate the Stoic virtues of wisdom, courage, justice, and moderation into your daily life. Think about how each of the virtues could manifest in the future you are aspiring to bring about. For example, what goals can contribute to added wisdom in your life? Are there areas of your life where you find yourself acting impulsively? It may be wiser, in certain instances, to stop and do things differently from time to time. How might you practice justice in order to contribute positively to the relationships you might hope to have with others? Are there aspects of your life where you find yourself giving 100% of yourself, and other areas that get neglected? Is there any way you can redress that imbalance?

Morris hoped to integrate courage, more than any other virtue, into his future. He wanted to face the void and uncertainty that was his retirement, and slowly fill it with new activities that could bring back balance and satisfaction into his life. To do so, and to grapple with the emotional and psychological distress he had already suffered, would take courage.

Step 2: Identifying Strengths and Limiting Beliefs

Recognize your strengths and weaknesses. Think about how can you leverage these strengths to overcome challenges and contribute to a meaningful life. When considering your weaknesses, identify and evaluate any limiting beliefs or negative thought patterns. Examine how these thoughts might hinder your pursuit of renewed purpose.

Morris saw his grit and determination, along with his fairly hard-nosed approach to most challenges, as some of his strengths. But although he could be fairly creative within the field of insurance and finance, he found himself to be lacking in imagination and spontaneity outside of it. However, he reframed this perceived lack of talent as an achievable goal to potentially work toward instead.

Step 3: Exploring Passions and Interests

Spend time scheduling and then testing out activities that you believe might bring you joy and fulfillment. When you have found some to be sufficiently engaging, consider which of those passions or interests align closely with your values and could thereby contribute to a meaningful life.

Step 4: Drafting a Mission Statement

Draft a concise mission statement that encapsulates your core values, life purpose, strengths, and commitment to more meaningful living. Compare your mission statement with your core values and principles, and check for alignment once again, to ensure that there are no unexpected clashes you may have unearthed in the drafting process. Check that your statement adheres to the Stoic virtue of moderation. Morris's own mission statement read as follows:

For decades, I applied my core values of hard work, perseverance, grit, and resilience to achieve success as an insurance industry stalwart. Now I am retired, I will find new avenues toward which I can direct the core values and skills I have developed, and by doing so will add new meaning to my life.

Step 5: Practicing Affirmations and Mindfulness

Develop positive affirmations based on your mission statement; these can be used to reinforce a positive mindset and guide your daily actions. Cultivate mindfulness in daily life so that you stay present and mindful, with a better ability to appreciate each moment as a measure of progress on your meaningful journey. Some of Morris' affirmations were the following:

I am hard working, and I know how to finish a task when I commit to it. I have always overcome the challenges I faced in the past. I will overcome them in the present and future as well.

Retirement is not an end, but a new beginning. It is a chance to open the door to a new activity. I will open that door and find something new to occupy my days and give my life meaning. There's some life in the old dog yet!

Step 6: Reviewing Your Mission Statement and Embracing Adaptability

Regularly review your mission statement and assess its impact on your thoughts and actions. Revise as needed to stay aligned with your evolving understanding of a meaningful life. Embrace the Stoic concepts of resilience and adaptability. If unforeseen setbacks or uncertainties are encountered when adhering to your mission statement, reframe them as opportunities for growth.

Morris: Finding a New Lease on Life

In the quiet of retirement, a Stoic spirit crafts not a lament for what was, but a purposeful melody for what can still be. –Unknown

In the process of setting new goals for himself to work toward, Morris was able to embrace retirement as an opportunity to create a meaningful and purposeful narrative for the next chapter of his life.

Inspired by some of the unfulfilled dreams he found in his journal, Morris tried his hand at several activities, such as gardening, fishing, and learning to play a musical instrument. Of these, he eventually settled on fishing and learning how to play the flute, even though he had practically no musical background whatsoever before he started.

Morris took up fishing as he had always loved the outdoors. It also appealed to his core values of persistence and commitment, and was an activity he felt he could learn to master at any age. In addition, Morris joined a fishing club in his town, which gave him an opportunity to widen his circle of friends and attend several fishing events organized by the club. This gave him a new lease on life, and strengthened his core value of friendship.

The flute was an instrument Morris had always wanted to play, and he did so as a kid but gave it up in favor of football—a more popular activity among his friends at the time. One afternoon, a neighbor told him about classes in folk music in the next town, which reminded him of this passion from long ago. Morris went along with his neighbor one evening and made the acquaintance of one of the organizers, who suggested he take up the flute in the beginners' adult class, which he did. Learning the flute aligned closely with his core values of mental stimulation, creativity, and persistence.

While connecting with a close friend and his family, Morris was asked his informed opinion by one of his friend's children on calculating financial risks and how to invest wisely in stocks. The young man then suggested Morris upload some long-form videos on YouTube about his knowledge of insurance policies and risk assessment, thereby introducing Morris to the uncharted world of vlogging—with the happy side benefit of allowing him to make use of the years of experience he had accumulated as a working professional.

He was slow to pick up on and improve in either of his newfound activities; however, both of them allowed Morris to approach them at his own pace and improve steadily over time, which aligned closely with his core values of hard work and commitment. Ultimately, Morris was able to fill the void in his life that had appeared after retirement. Some of the dreams he had written down in his journal would remain unfulfilled, but by embracing the present with the aid of Stoic principles, Morris found new ones to add the meaning and purpose to his life that he had sorely missed.

Chapter 5:

Virtue as the Highest Good

It is not that we seek to avoid the void, but that we fill it with virtue and purpose. – Unknown

We are faced with many ethical decisions and challenges every day, from the smallest of considerations to the toughest of choices. For the Stoics, these moments are important as they are opportunities to practice virtue and flourish. These challenges are what are referred to as "the void"; to fill it with virtue and purpose is to respond to difficulty with principled actions and a firm purpose. Sarah found herself presented with such an opportunity to demonstrate virtue during a conflict of interest at her workplace.

Sarah worked as a senior project manager for a construction company, overseeing various development projects. One day, she was assigned to manage a high-profile selection process for a new client who was a close friend of her immediate supervisor, David. The project was crucial for the company's financial success, and the client had expressed a desire for favorable terms.

As Sarah delved into the project, she discovered that there was a subcontractor bidding process underway. However, she soon learned that David had a personal connection with one of the subcontractors, and he strongly recommended awarding this particular subcontractor the contract. Sarah was aware that the subcontractor in question, while competent, proposed a disproportionately high pricing policy relative to the other bidders.

Sarah therefore found herself facing a conflict of interest. On the one hand, she wanted to maintain a positive relationship with her supervisor, David, who had a significant influence over her career progression. On the other hand, she recognized her responsibility to act in the best interests of the company, which included ensuring that fair and cost-effective subcontractors were selected for the company's projects.

Ethical Considerations

If it is not right, do not do it. If it is not true, do not say it. —Marcus Aurelius

Sarah needed to navigate more than one ethical dilemma during this situation. There was, of course, the personal conflict of interest between her loyalty to her supervisor and her duty to act in the best interests of the company. Similarly, the principles of fairness and integrity dictated that the company's well-being took precedence over personal relationships, particularly when it came to financial transactions on behalf of the company.

However, Sarah also needed to consider how transparent and open she should be about her knowledge of the personal connection between David and the subcontractor. In addition, there were also the company's own core values and ethical guidelines to take into account; as an employee, Sarah was obliged to align her decisions with the values upheld by the organization.

Sarah also had to consider possible resolutions, as well as backup plans in the event that certain resolutions were not as effective as expected. For instance, she could communicate her concerns about the potential conflict of interest to David openly, and seek a resolution that prioritized the company's best interests.

However, if the issue persisted in spite of her concerns being raised, Sarah would need to escalate the matter to higher management, or even the Conduct and Compliance Department, to ensure a fair and unbiased decision-making process. She hoped it would not come to that, though, as either process would indicate that matters were possibly graver than she had anticipated them to be.

Sarah's turmoil illustrates the complexity of ethical dilemmas, especially those involving conflicts of interest. Individuals like Sarah often grapple with the challenge of balancing personal relationships with professional responsibilities, highlighting the importance of ethical decision-making in the workplace.

Understanding Stoic Virtue Ethics

The wise man is neither raised up by prosperity nor cast down by adversity. – Seneca

There are many different types of ethical systems. Consequentialist ethics keeps an eye on the outcome of any particular action, reasoning that what is ethical is what provides the best result. Rule-based ethics focuses on a set of specific precepts, arguing that it is imperative to follow these rules, even if they sometimes lead to worse consequences. Lastly, virtue ethics focuses on the state of mind behind your action and whether it was undertaken with the proper motivations, regardless of any particular precept or outcome. As has been covered previously in this book, Stoicism has a type of virtue ethics at the core of its mindset.

Since it is not a rule-based ethics system, Stoicism isn't about a set of immovable precepts that direct your every action; it has a larger focus on analyzing a situation and thinking for yourself. So much depends on specific factors and the context, and you must consider your situation with respect to your own understanding of virtue. In this manner, however you choose to react, you will know that you tried to act virtuously and with integrity. And, after the event has passed, you will be able to self-reflect and judge if there are any lessons to be learned from the experience.

Sarah applied each of the four Stoic virtues to her own situation when contemplating the best course of action for her to take:

Wisdom

The ancient Greeks differentiated between two kinds of wisdom: *sophia*, which is general wisdom, and *phronesis*, which is practical wisdom. The Stoics embraced the latter as a cardinal virtue. In navigating her ethical dilemma, Sarah applied practical wisdom by carefully considering the consequences of her actions and making decisions that aligned with the broader goals, values, and virtues of the company. This ensured that her choices contributed to the overall well-being and success of the organization.

Courage

This was also referred to as *andreia* by the ancient Stoics. To address the conflict of interest, Sarah needed moral courage to stand firm with honesty and integrity in her commitment to the company's best interests, even if it meant confronting her supervisor and challenging his recommendation for the subcontractor.

Justice

The virtue of justice, or *dikaiosyne* in ancient Greek, guided Sarah to prioritize fairness in her decision-making. She wanted to ensure that the subcontractor selection process was fair and in alignment with the ethical standards upheld by the company, thereby acting with a sense of duty to the company's stakeholders.

Moderation

This was called *sophrosyne* by the Stoics. In her actions and communications, Sarah exercised moderation and restraint to avoid impulsive reactions or confrontations. She maintained her focus on the actions and decisions themselves, and cast no judgment on the people involved. Due to the sensitive nature of the situation, this level of thoughtfulness was needed to avert any unnecessary conflicts while still conveying the importance of ethical decision-making.

In adopting a Stoic mindset, Sarah recognized the aspects beyond her control, such as the personal connection between David and the subcontractor. As such, she instead turned her attention toward the inherent virtue in her own actions when facing the dilemma. Sarah found solace in the fact that she was acting in accordance with wisdom, courage, justice, and moderation, irrespective of the challenges she faced from her supervisor and the organization. In addition, by aligning her actions with Stoic virtues, Sarah cultivated inner strength and tranquility, which helped her to make peace with the situation in her own way, regardless of her external circumstances and relations.

Applying Virtue to Everyday Choices

We should every night call ourselves to an account: What infirmity have I mastered today? What passions opposed? What temptation resisted? What virtue acquired?
—Seneca

Virtue can be defined as the art of living in harmony with the world. A central tenet of Stoicism is that living in accordance with your principles is the key to achieving *eudaimonia*, a state of flourishing and a fulfilled life. In other words, the key to a good, happy life is to act virtuously in all circumstances.

The ancient Greeks held that philosophy was the study of how to live a good life, and so started by seeking to define what they meant by "good." The Stoics reasoned that the ultimate good must be something that is always good, rather than something that is only contextually so. For example, wealth is not always good—if you are addicted to harmful narcotics, coming into sudden wealth could be ruinous—so it follows that wealth cannot be the true good.

These kinds of considerations led the Stoics to consider the virtues. By its nature, virtue is always good regardless of the context, so the virtues are the "true good" that underpin a good life. Instead of being motivated primarily by wealth, or some other contextual good, the Stoics therefore held that one should be motivated primarily by what is virtuous.

The fundamental, empowering thing about this idea is that it's always under your control whether you act virtuously. If bad things happen to you, you can still choose to react virtuously. And, because the key to a good life is simply to be virtuous, it follows that you can have a good life regardless of what happens to you. You can achieve your own state of *eudaimonia* even in the most difficult circumstances, and flourish under adversity—all by integrating virtue into your everyday actions and choices. As Marcus Aurelius (161–180/2006) wrote: "If at some point, you should come across anything better than justice, wisdom, discipline, courage—it must be an extraordinary thing indeed."

Integrating virtue into everyday life choices holds significant value as it contributes significantly to personal well-being and the cultivation of a positive and meaningful life. Virtues provide a moral compass that can guide you in making ethical decisions. This helps you navigate complex situations with clarity and integrity. Living in alignment with the virtues fosters a sense of purpose and fulfillment, contributing to a deeper satisfaction with life. Consistently practicing deeds that are aligned with good motivations is an effective way to develop and strengthen character. This, in turn, influences how you are perceived by others and contributes to positive relationships with them. Sarah's adoption of virtue in her thinking and actions allowed her to navigate her ethical dilemma with poise and integrity, while still maintaining the good working relationships she had with her supervisor and the company she worked for.

As previous chapters have shown, certain virtues such as courage and resilience empower you to face challenges with fortitude, bounce back from setbacks, and maintain emotional well-being. Virtuous actions also inspire and uplift those around you, fostering a positive and supportive community. Acts of kindness, empathy, and justice contribute to a harmonious social environment. These actions can also help promote and project authenticity, and foster a sense of coherence in your beliefs and behaviors through the act of aligning your actions with your core values. Finally, living virtuously contributes to inner peace and tranquility. By focusing on virtues, you can navigate life's uncertainties with a sense of calm and acceptance. The following practices are some ways to integrate virtue into everyday life:

Reflecting on Values and Intentions

Regularly take time to reflect on your core values and beliefs. Before making decisions, no matter how insignificant, set your intentions to be based on virtues. Consider how your choices align with your core values and principles you may hold in high regard, such as honesty, kindness, and justice.

Practicing Mindfulness and Discussing Virtue Ethics

Mindful awareness allows you to pause and consider the virtuous implications of your choices. And by discussing virtue ethics with friends, family, or colleagues, you can deepen your understanding and reinforce the importance of virtues in decision-making. Identify role models who exemplify virtues you admire. Learn from their behaviors and incorporate similar virtues into your own life.

Creating Virtue-Based Habits

Whether it's acts of kindness, resilience-building exercises, or moments of gratitude, making these virtuous actions a habit reinforces their integration into daily life. In addition, prioritize self-care as a virtuous act; it is important to maintain your well-being and emotional health as a foundation for principled living. When acknowledging past mistakes and learning from them, reflect on how virtues can guide improved choices in similar situations in future.

By consciously integrating principles into everyday choices, you can lead a more intentional, purposeful, and honorable life. This not only contributes to personal growth but also fosters a positive impact on your surrounding community and society at large. By integrating Stoic virtues into her decision-making process, Sarah was guided by principles that transcended her personal interests and relationships, ultimately contributing to a workplace environment grounded in Stoic virtue.

Sarah: Embracing Fairness With Integrity

In the crossroads of conflicting interests, a Stoic heart navigates not by the allure of gain but by the compass of virtue, for true wealth lies in the integrity of one's choices.
—Unknown

Sarah approached her conflict of interest with a focus on principled choices rather than short-term gains, and emphasized the value of integrity and ethical decision-making. In the end, Sarah chose a path aligned with the best interests of the company and its stakeholders.

Sarah, embracing wisdom, carefully considered the consequences of her actions and the impact on the company's success. With moral courage, she addressed the conflict openly, conveying her concerns about the subcontractor selection process to her supervisor, David.

Guided by the virtue of justice, Sarah advocated for fairness, ensuring that the subcontractor selection was based on merit and aligned with the ethical standards of the company. She navigated the delicate situation with moderation, maintaining a composed and thoughtful approach in her communication with David.

For her efforts and in appreciation of her measured actions to address the issue, David responded by withdrawing his push for his personal recommendation for the subcontractor contract. The company proceeded with the bidding process, and screened all applications with fairness and integrity, including David's own recommended subcontractor. While Sarah was not publicly acknowledged for her part in this, she had reached a stage where external validation was not necessary: Her actions were aligned with her values, and that was sufficient validation for her.

Sarah's commitment to Stoic virtues remained unwavering. Her choice reflected a dedication to ethical conduct and a steadfast pursuit of excellence in both her personal and professional life. In aligning her decisions with Stoic principles, Sarah aimed to contribute to a workplace culture rooted in virtue, resilience, and a commitment to the greater good. The conclusion of her story highlights the enduring impact of Stoic ethics in guiding individuals through challenging ethical dilemmas.

Chapter 6:

Managing Anger and Negative Emotions

The best revenge is to be unlike him who performed the injustice. –Marcus Aurelius

A common misconception is that expressing aggression has cathartic value: that by hitting the horn, or punching a pillow, you can "get it out of your system" or otherwise temper your aggression. However, modern psychology doesn't back this up. A study at Iowa State University found that cathartic actions like punching a pillow do nothing to dispel your anger, and may even encourage you to more aggressive behaviors in the future (Bushman, 2002).

Anger isn't something to be ignored, but it is something to be mastered. It's okay to acknowledge that your first emotional reaction to a certain set of circumstances is irritation; this is part of understanding your own nature, giving you wisdom and insight into your own behaviors. However, to then act on that anger aggressively goes against the virtues of wisdom and moderation. At best, aggression will indulge those negative feelings of anger, rather than help you to process them. At worst, it may lead to a verbal or physical confrontation with a stranger.

Emma had the same issues to navigate when she found herself feeling angry and frustrated with not just one, but two separate challenges she faced in her life. With the help of Stoicism, she was able to prevent these external troubles from dictating her own actions, and thereby avoided acting with aggression or rage in a way that would have caused irreparable damage to both her professional and personal life.

Emma's Workplace Challenges

He who is not a good servant will not be a good master. —Seneca

Emma was a talented software developer working for a tech company. She was passionate about her work and strived to meet project deadlines. However, during a recent trying stretch of weeks, she faced numerous challenges, including unrealistic project timelines, changing requirements, and an increased workload due to staff reductions. These challenges led to frequent frustrations and bouts of anger in the workplace.

When Emma consistently received project timelines that were unrealistic, it led to her being burdened by pressure and stress. When the project requirements she was subject to changed, they did so often and abruptly, requiring Emma to adapt quickly and perform tasks on the fly; this in turn impacted the quality of her work. The cost-cutting measures that led to staff reductions also indirectly caused an increase in Emma's workload, making it challenging for her to maintain a healthy work–life balance. In addition, she felt that communication within the team had become insufficient, leading to misunderstandings that further aggravated her own frustrations.

These frustrations peaked when she perceived her efforts as undervalued by the rest of her team, and she struggled to express her concerns effectively. The pent-up frustration and anger she felt due to her situation had a deteriorating effect on Emma's overall job satisfaction, productivity, and relationships with colleagues.

Strategies for Emotional Self-Control

The nearer a man comes to a calm mind, the closer he is to strength. —Marcus Aurelius

In Emma's case, Stoicism offered valuable principles to navigate frustration and anger while maintaining a sense of agency over her reactions. This was due to Stoicism's emphasis on the development of inner resilience, focusing on what is within one's control, and responding mindfully to external challenges.

While Emma did not have control over external factors like project timelines, she could control her responses, her communication, and how she approached the challenges she was facing. As for the external events beyond her control, such as the shifting project requirements and increased workload, Emma acknowledged them as being a part of the job, and that she still had the power to adjust her own reactions to those conditions.

Emma developed resilience by viewing the challenges she faced as opportunities for personal growth and learning, and by reframing her perspective on the various setbacks to a more positive one. She integrated mindfulness techniques, such as meditation and PMR, into her daily routine to help her manage frustration by helping her stay focused on the current task rather than becoming overwhelmed by future uncertainties.

The Stoics valued patience, and saw it not as passive acceptance of one's circumstances, but instead as an active, disciplined waiting for the right moment to act. By adopting the same perspective, Emma was able to navigate through her anger and anxieties with a calm and composed demeanor. For instance, before responding to frustrating situations, she learned to take a moment to pause and reflect. This brief interruption allowed her to choose a deliberate and measured action to take instead of reacting impulsively.

The act of pausing and reflecting is one of many techniques that enabled Emma to develop better self-control and manage her resentment toward her situation:

Setting Realistic Expectations

Emma set realistic expectations for herself and others in her team. This involved recognizing her own limitations, communicating effectively about project timelines, and negotiating for deadlines that aligned with an output of higher quality work.

Developing Emotional Intelligence

Working to enhance her emotional intelligence enabled Emma to understand and manage her emotions more effectively. This involved recognizing triggers, learning to express her feelings constructively, and practicing empathy. The latter gave her a chance to step back, take a breather and view the situation from different perspectives—those of her employer, her colleagues, and her wise parent.

Utilizing Stoic Affirmations

Emma incorporated Stoic affirmations into her daily routine. She regularly reminded herself of Stoic principles such as acceptance of external events, the dichotomy of control, and the importance of virtuous actions and thoughts, all of which contributed toward the resilience of her mindset:

I commit to effective communication and setting boundaries. By expressing my concerns assertively and establishing clear communication channels within the team, I create a foundation for understanding and collaboration. I recognize that open dialogue is essential for a healthy work environment.

Engaging in Cognitive Restructuring

Cognitive restructuring involves reframing negative thought patterns. Emma examined and then challenged the more irrational beliefs she had that were contributing to her frustration, and replaced them with more rational and constructive perspectives. For example, she challenged the notion that she was incapable of supporting her increased workload, and instead reframed it as an opportunity to improve her workplace methods. She created a spreadsheet listing all of her tasks and projects with timelines, progress, and details on any delays and shared this with her manager on a monthly basis. She later rolled this out across the team to get greater visibility of the team workload and progress. She also discussed the possibility of automating certain repetitive tasks with her IT support staff.

Emma: Initiating Change

Amidst workplace trials and tribulations, a Stoic spirit rises not in the storms of anger but in the cultivation of resilience, turning challenges into opportunities for serene strength. –Unknown

By integrating Stoic principles and adopting strategies for maintaining self-control, Emma was able to navigate her workplace challenges with resilience and a virtuous mindset. This approach empowered her to respond with composure to the frustration and anger she felt, which ultimately contributed to a more constructive and fulfilling work experience.

Emma first reached out to HR as well as a former supervisor and mentor of hers to discuss her workload concerns and explore potential solutions. She also explored stress management and coping techniques to handle frustration and anger more effectively. Her mentor recommended some workshops on emotional intelligence that she eventually attended. From the workshops, Emma picked up on mindfulness practices she could incorporate into her routine, such as meditation and deep breathing exercises, to help manage her stress and cultivate a calmer mindset in challenging situations.

Recognizing the need for change, and determined to address her workplace challenges, Emma decided to take a proactive approach. She initiated an open and honest conversation with her manager, expressing her concerns about the unrealistic project timelines, changing project parameters, and increased workload affecting the well-being of both her and the team.

In the meeting, Emma highlighted specific instances where the workload was overwhelming and provided data on the impact it had on the team's productivity. She also set clear boundaries regarding the abilities of herself and her team, and communicated the need for more realistic project planning to ensure quality work and employee well-being.

Surprisingly, her manager, though initially resistant, listened attentively to Emma's points. Emma proposed a collaborative effort to re-evaluate project timelines, redistribute tasks more evenly among team members, and establish a more open communication channel to address concerns promptly.

Seeing the genuine concern from Emma, and recognizing the potential benefits of a more balanced and supportive work environment, the manager agreed to implement changes. Together, they worked on restructuring project timelines, providing additional resources where needed, and fostering a culture of open communication within the team.

Meanwhile, Emma and her team collaboratively identified areas for improvement in the project management process. This involved implementing changes that reduced the sudden requirement shifts in projects, and enhanced intra-team communication.

As a result, the workplace atmosphere gradually improved. Team members felt more supported, and the quality of work increased. Emma's proactive approach not only addressed her own frustration but also contributed to positive changes benefiting the entire team. Seeking support, mindfulness practices, open communication, boundary-setting, skill development, and collaborative problem-solving all collectively contributed to addressing and mitigating the challenges associated with frustration and anger in the workplace. The experience taught Emma the importance of advocating for oneself and initiating constructive conversations to bring about positive workplace transformations.

However, Emma's difficulties with negative emotions such as frustration and anger were not quite resolved yet...

Emma's Relationship Struggles

Any person capable of angering you becomes your master; he can anger you only when you permit yourself to be disturbed by him. —Epictetus

Emma has been married to Mark for seven years, and, during that time, she has noticed a significant shift in their relationship dynamics. Mark, once supportive and engaged, has gradually become emotionally distant. They shared the responsibilities of raising their two young children, but Emma often found herself overwhelmed as Mark consistently passed most of the workload back to her. This felt doubly burdensome given the troubles she was simultaneously facing at her workplace.

Despite numerous requests to share their responsibilities, Emma's pleas seemed to fall on deaf ears, and she constantly found herself eventually doing the majority of the work. Additionally, Mark refused to engage in open discussions about the issues Emma raised, going so far as to claim that there were no problems in their relationship. He attended two counseling sessions but adamantly refused to continue, leaving Emma feeling stuck and unsupported.

Techniques for Managing Anger and Negative Emotions

Steel your sensibilities, so that life shall hurt you as little as possible. —Zeno of Citium (In R. Holiday & S. Hanselman, 2016)

To understand how the Stoics approached anger, it's worth understanding a little more about their philosophy. Seneca (c.65/2018) wrote that human action is best understood as assent or dissent (i.e., agreement or disagreement) to certain "impressions," where those impressions are immediate, emotional responses to external events.

Seneca argued that, as a rational human being, you have the choice of whether you assent or dissent to those immediate impressions. In other words, you get to choose whether or not you act on an impression of anger and aggression, for instance. This is where you can apply reason: the consideration of virtue and what it means to live a good life.

It's a common misunderstanding that Stoicism advocates an unfeeling or robotic way of life. That's why it's important to understand the idea of impressions and assent/dissent. Stoicism doesn't ask you to be unfeeling; it makes space for those initial impressions where your emotions and feelings are felt. However, Stoicism *does* ask you to apply reason to those immediate, emotional responses, and to choose whether or not it is virtuous to act on those feelings.

Of course, it is often easier said than done to keep your emotions under control. This is why it's important to take a breath, so that there's time for you to choose whether to assent or dissent to your impressions. If you don't take that breath, you may act on autopilot, going from your impressions to immediate action, and behave in a way that is unwise and hot-headed. Emma adopted this as the "pause and reflect" technique in her workplace, and found it just as useful for dealing with her circumstances closer to home.

Other techniques covered in this book that require you to pause for a moment and think about your situation, such as the 4–7–8 breathing technique and self-reflection, are also effective in curbing impulses toward anger and aggression. Along with these, the following techniques that Emma eventually adopted can also help temper and manage your own negative emotions:

Progressive Muscle Relaxation

The basic idea behind PMR is to tense and then deliberately relax each part of your body in succession. This is related to anger, as a very common physical sensation associated with this emotion is tension in the muscles or jaw. Not only is this tension *associated* with anger, but—as expressed by the cognitive cycle of CBT—that tension *contributes* to the emotion of anger as well. Therefore, relieving this tension can help reduce your anger.

First, find somewhere comfortable and quiet where you can sit or lie down on your back. If you choose to sit, make sure your feet are touching the floor and your back is straight and supported. Then, take a few deep breaths to get yourself in the right mindset. The 4–7–8 breathing technique can be used effectively here.

Starting with your feet, gently bring your attention to each part of your body—begin with the toes on one foot, then move to the sole of the foot, then the heel, and so on. At each part of the body, do the following:

1. Bring your awareness to any sensations you are experiencing at that body part, such as feelings of tension, contact with other objects, or the temperature that it is at.

2. Tense the muscles in that part of the body, and hold that tension for a few seconds. Try to tense only the muscles in the body part that you're focusing on. Throughout the tensing, pay attention to how it feels, and take care not to overdo it and cause an injury to that body part.

3. After holding the tension for a few seconds, deliberately relax the muscles in that body part. Pay attention to how different it feels from before, and bring your awareness to that new, relaxed sensation for 10 seconds or so.

4. Then, gently redirect your attention to another part of your body, moving from one foot to the other, or upward into your calves, and so on.

When you have completed steps 1 to 4 above for your entire body, take a few more deep breaths to recenter yourself—the 4–7–8 breathing exercise can again be utilized here. Bring your awareness back to your surroundings, and you should be able to continue your day in relative calm.

PMR is best practiced habitually. Habitual PMR helps train your mind to notice when you feel tense, giving you an opportunity to deliberately relax your muscles and avoid feelings of anger. Moreover, habitual PMR helps regulate your emotions by giving you space in the day to relax and reflect on them. During PMR, if your attention ever drifts to another part of your body, simply acknowledge that your attention has drifted and gently bring it back to where it should be focused.

Recontextualization

Another useful technique for dealing with anger inspired by Stoicism is to deliberately reflect on alternative ways to think about the source of your anger. Recontextualization works best when written down, as writing helps focus your mind.

To begin, write down what's made you angry. You can incorporate CBT techniques here, by outlining your patterns of thought, behavior, emotions, and physical feelings revolving around what has made you angry. If another person has made you angry, give an account of the same event from their perspective. Be as objective and empathetic as you can, and focus more on the task of placing yourself in their shoes than on being very accurate with the answers. Ask yourself questions such as:

What was their intention in this situation?

If I did what they did, how would I expect them to react?

What would be a good reaction in that situation, when seeing it from the other person's perspective?

Meanwhile, if the situation doesn't involve another person, reflect on learning opportunities from the experience. Recontextualization is helpful because it takes you outside of your own head just when you're most susceptible to act on your immediate impressions. It can also help build empathy and greater understanding of your fellow humans.

Other Techniques for Managing Anger and Negativity

> *In the shadows of unsupportive realms, a Stoic heart finds not despair, but the luminance of self-reliance, turning solitude into the sanctuary of resilient inner strength.* –Unknown

Fundamentally, the key to challenging anger is to recognize that it is rarely useful. Meditating on this truth can help you make better choices, especially if you reflect on the uselessness of anger on a habitual basis. Emma saw this as the dual nature of anger: While it can motivate us, it can also drain us. Expressing anger generally provokes further anger, which makes achieving a compromise more challenging. Anger also clouds our judgment, hindering our ability to see potential solutions.

To give in to anger and to act on impulse is to give up your inherent humanity. After all, you are a rational creature, capable of assenting or dissenting to your impressions, as Seneca put it. If you give in to anger, you're acting immediately on your impressions without applying that rational choice that makes you human. In this way, giving in to anger is unjust to yourself. You give up control, because your impressions are immediate and automatic, and you become enslaved to those angry emotions. So, it isn't just that anger can lead you to act in ways that cause problems; giving into your anger is unfair to your own inherent nature.

Acceptance of Control

Embrace the reality that some events are beyond your influence, and focus on your response to situations rather than the situations themselves. Emma used this to detach her own reactions from Mark's unhelpful behavior. She recentered herself and focused on expanding her own circle of influence. Embracing this notion gave her more peace of mind and further distanced her actions from Mark's as a short-term self-protective measure.

Reframing Negative Thought Patterns

Identify negative thoughts that often arise regarding the source of the anger. For every thought, examine evidence that either supports or contradicts it. Use these findings to formulate a more balanced, realistic perspective to replace the negative thought. For example, Emma changed her thought of *I am stuck* to *I can work my way out of this feeling of being stuck*. When Emma noticed herself being triggered, she mentally visualized a huge sign saying "STOP!". This helped her to retreat from pointless situations. She found that choosing her battles was wiser and helped her conserve and use her energy more constructively. Use this same technique to practice self-compassion by replacing negative beliefs with positive affirmations, such as, "I am doing my best, and that is enough."

Being Grateful

Take a few minutes daily to write down three things you're grateful for. Be specific, and focus on both big and small aspects of your life. The shift in focus to positive aspects fosters a more optimistic mindset that is less prone to anger and negativity. Emma was grateful for her two children, the roof over her head, and her own physical health.

Seeing the Bigger Picture

Consider the temporary nature of circumstances and emotions. Reflect on how current challenges appear in the broader context of your life. Then bring your attention back to the present moment. Mindfully engage in activities without dwelling on past regrets or fearing future uncertainties. This kind of broad view and shift in perspective helped Emma to maintain emotional balance during the difficulties she faced with Mark.

Self-Soothing Visualizations and Anticipating Setbacks

Take a minute to close your eyes and vividly imagine a peaceful, positive scene. Engage all your senses in the visualization—imagine how elements in the scene might smell, sound, or feel. Practice this visualization regularly to create a mental refuge during moments of stress.

At the same time, contemplate potential challenges and setbacks before they occur. Visualize worst-case scenarios (*premeditatio malorum*, or "premeditation of adversity") and mentally prepare for them. This helps you desensitize yourself to fear and reduces the impact of negative surprises. Remember to practice *amor fati*, or "love of fate," and embrace both positive and negative outcomes as a part of life's journey.

Prioritizing Tasks

Break tasks into smaller, manageable steps. Prioritize these based on their urgency and importance. Completing tasks systematically in this manner reduces stress and feelings of being overwhelmed. Emma used this technique to make her household chores easier to manage. She decided to delegate many of her low-priority and repetitive household or administrative tasks to others.

Seeking Support From Friends and Family

Share your feelings with a trusted friend or family member. Discussing emotions with others provides support and alternative, fresh perspectives. This is partly why a strong support system is crucial for emotional well-being.

Taking Time Out for Physical Activity

Engage in activities you enjoy, whether it's walking, jogging, or dancing. Physical exercise releases endorphins, improving mood and reducing stress. Aim for at least 30 minutes of moderate exercise most days. Emma took up jogging for 30–45 minutes on weekdays.

Emma: Forging a New Path

At the crossroads of endurance, a Stoic soul contemplates not perpetual suffering, but the courage to forge a new path, transforming an end into the genesis of resilient self-discovery. –Unknown

Facing Mark's refusal to continue counseling, Emma decided to prioritize her own well-being. She acknowledged that she couldn't force Mark to change, but she could still decide her own response to the situation. Emma sought individual therapy to explore coping strategies and gain support in navigating the challenges within her marriage.

By integrating Stoic principles and CBT strategies, Emma empowered herself to focus on personal growth, manage her emotional responses, and take practical steps to address the dynamics in her relationship. This combined approach provided a balanced framework for navigating her challenges while fostering resilience and self-empowerment.

Recognizing the need for change and improvement of her own well-being, Emma initiated a calm and focused conversation with Mark, clearly expressing her feelings and needs, and the impact of the unequal distribution of responsibilities on their relationship. Despite Mark's initial resistance and denial of any issues, Emma remained steadfast in her commitment to positive change. Drawing on Stoic principles, she accepted that Mark might not see the problems in the same way initially, but she remained patient and persistent in her communication. Emma continued to implement CBT strategies as well, challenging negative thought patterns and setting clear boundaries.

In the process, Mark began to witness the positive changes in Emma's demeanor and the constructive approach she adopted. He started to recognize the impact of his actions on the relationship. This realization prompted Mark to reconsider his stance.

Eventually, the couple decided to attend counseling together again. With the guidance of a professional, they engaged in open discussions, addressing underlying issues and working on effective communication. Mark, acknowledging the need for shared responsibilities, actively participated in restructuring their roles within the relationship.

The marriage underwent a transformative phase as both partners committed to understanding each other better and fostering a more supportive and balanced dynamic. Emma's resilience, coupled with the principles of Stoicism and CBT, not only improved her individual well-being but also contributed to positive changes in the overall health of their relationship.

While challenges remained, the couple developed a more collaborative and understanding approach, recognizing the ongoing nature of growth and improvement in any relationship. Emma's story concluded with her feeling more empowered, supported, and optimistic about the future of her marriage.

Chapter 7:

Dealing With Change and Transition

He who fears death will never do anything worthy of a man who is alive. —Seneca

Many life transitions are happy events, such as new relationships, marriage, or having a baby. These important events can have a profound influence on your everyday life. Though it may take some time to fully adjust to such a big change, these kinds of transitions are relatively easy to embrace since they are caused by something that is fundamentally positive. However, some life transitions are not so positive, such as the loss of a job, a forced move to a different location, or a divorce and its fallout. These life events can be just as disruptive to your everyday life, but they are much harder to embrace as the opportunities they represent.

Mia faced such a major life transition when she and her family moved to Europe from the US. Seneca's musings above indirectly inspired her to approach the big change with courage and a focus on the opportunities for growth and enrichment that the new experience in Europe potentially offered.

The reason Mia and her family embarked on such a significant life change was that Mia's husband received a three-year work assignment in France. This opportunity marked a crucial step toward his senior management aspirations. Since they were based in the US, Mia faced the challenge of uprooting her family and adapting to a new culture and language across the Atlantic.

The prospect of the transition brought to light several challenges and concerns. Mia and her children had limited proficiency in French and were unfamiliar with the local customs in the area they were moving to. Mia had a fulfilling job herself in the US, but as it did not allow for her to work remotely, Mia was forced to navigate sacrifices and other changes to her professional life. And the transition posed challenges for the children in adapting to a new school, making new friends, and adjusting to a different cultural environment—and Mia would need to be there to face those challenges with them.

Embracing Change

> *Very little is needed to make a happy life; it is all within yourself, in your way of thinking.* –Marcus Aurelius

The Stoics recognized that change is natural, and that all states are transitional. As Marcus Aurelius (161–180/2008) said, "Everything you see will alter and cease to exist. Think of how many changes you've already seen; the world is nothing but change." Not only is change a part of life, but it's also a fundamentally important aspect of any human endeavor—consider how everything you do causes something, somewhere to change, no matter how insignificant that change may be.

Aurelius went on to demonstrate this through basic examples, such as burning wood for a hot bath and consuming food for nutrition. In either case, something changes in order for a useful outcome (i.e., cleanliness and nourishment) to be achieved. In this sense, then, change is to be embraced, because nothing can be achieved without change. Though some changes may bring hardship, it's important to recognize that this is part of the rich tapestry of life and the cosmos.

Acceptance of change, however, is not the same as responding passively to it. Stoicism always advocates for actively seeking out opportunities for personal growth and improvement: In the words of Seneca (c.65/2018), "As each day arises, welcome it as the very best day of all, and make it your own possession. We must seize what flees." This applies to life transitions as well; to lead a worthy life, seize every opportunity that change brings, no matter the size or impact of the change. While Mia was perfectly happy living in the US and had never envisaged moving abroad herself, she acknowledged that this promotion would dramatically improve the fortunes of her husband and family and thus fundamentally supported the change.

Practical Measures for Navigating Transitions

In the voyage of change, a Stoic heart embraces not the fear of the unknown, but the sails of resilience, navigating transitions as opportunities to unfurl the canvas of a purposeful journey. –Unknown

To see how Stoic principles can be applied to embracing change and transition, let us look at the various practical measures and steps Mia took to make the most out of her move to France with her family:

Adopting a Stoic Mindset

Mia started by rationally reflecting on her experiences and the challenges to come, with an eye on opportunities for personal growth and improvement. She internalized and accepted the nature of external events: that some of them were beyond her control, and that change is a constant aspect of life. She acknowledged the emotions she was feeling about the upcoming move, and did not allow them to dominate her thinking. Instead, she worked to reframe her more negative thoughts and beliefs, and by doing so developed a more optimistic and positive mindset that was focused on learning, adaptability, and the maintenance of inner tranquility. Mia embraced the uncertainty and nervousness she was feeling and knew she could not micromanage every challenge that might come their way.

This eventually led to Mia looking into and signing up her family for basic French language courses in the US to help facilitate their initial adjustment to their new life.

Setting Expectations and Creating an Action Plan

When Mia thought about the aspects of her situation that she could and couldn't control, she began to set realistic expectations and goals for herself, and then created an action plan based on those expectations and goals. Mia also practiced both positive and negative visualizations to help prepare her mind for all the potential challenges their family might face in the new environment, thereby improving her ability to maintain tranquility and inner strength in the face of challenges. During this process, she constantly checked that her expectations and actions were aligned with the Stoic virtues and core values she held close to her heart: wisdom, moderation, family bonds, community relationships, and togetherness.

Some of the preliminary actions that Mia engaged in as part of her plan included research on life in France, local customs, and educational opportunities for her children.

Communicating Effectively

To help maintain emotional resilience, as well as to stay present and mindful of her circumstances, Mia prioritized improving communication with her family and friends to strengthen her personal relationships. Mia and her husband established open communication about their individual concerns and expectations during the transition, and they implemented and actively engaged in regular family meetings with their children to discuss progress, challenges, and emotions.

Building a Support System and Prioritizing Self-Care

Mia considered community and social relationships as some of her core values, so she needed very little extra incentive to work toward building a social support network to help her family navigate this new challenge. She sought out expat communities and support groups in France to connect with others going through similar experiences, and encouraged her husband to engage with colleagues who had prior experience of working in France for valuable insights. Mia also focused on looking after her physical and mental health to ensure she was in good condition for any trials ahead. She tried to focus on activities such as jogging and yoga that were easily transferable to the new location.

Staying Flexible and Exploring New Perspectives

As part of her efforts to further develop her Stoic mindset, Mia tried to improve how flexible and adaptable she was in response to external events, how quickly and effectively she could reflect and learn from those events, and how consciously she could come up with new approaches to help navigate her circumstances.

A large part of this revolved around Mia's need to change jobs to facilitate the move. So, she explored potential professional opportunities in France, with a focus on remote work or part-time engagements. She also leveraged her existing network for potential connections or recommendations in the local job market, and even looked into adjacent jobs in similar fields that she might be qualified to apply for.

Celebrating Victories and Maintaining Positivity

Mia acknowledged the value of celebrating and recognizing progress and achievements, no matter how small in scope, as part of the journey toward more virtuous living. She saw that this also supported her goal of developing a more optimistic and positive mindset. Some of the wins that she celebrated included reaching progress milestones in her French lessons—not only hers, but those of her family as well.

In essence, the practical steps above can guide you through the external events revolving around a life transition with resilience, wisdom, and a focus on virtuous living. By following the above, Mia was able to approach the change in her life with resilience and purpose, along with curiosity and a proactive mindset, and to reframe and approach the transition as a chance to explore new possibilities and cultivate personal growth. She therefore aligned herself with the Stoic principle of embracing change as a catalyst for self-discovery and resilience.

Mia: Adapting to a New Life

> *In the landscape of change, a Stoic spirit plants not roots in resistance, but seeds of curiosity, cultivating opportunities to bloom in the vast garden of self-discovery.* –
> Unknown

As Mia's family embarked on their journey to France, the initial months brought both challenges and opportunities. However, the family had diligently prepared for the transition, with Mia leading the way in implementing strategies to make the relocation as smooth as possible.

Mia and the children engaged in French language courses and cultural activities. Over time, their proficiency improved, to the point that when they reached France they were already quite knowledgeable, with many basic phrases and essential vocabulary. This helped them to more readily foster a sense of connection with the local community.

With a strong Stoic-enhanced determination to adapt professionally, Mia continued to explore remote work opportunities after the move, and discovered a vibrant job market that she was qualified to enter. She leveraged her network to secure a part-time English-speaking role that allowed her to balance her career aspirations with family priorities.

Due to Mia's push for better social connectivity and togetherness, the family actively participated in expat events in the city they moved to, building a strong support network in their new home. Mia's husband forged and maintained connections with some of his colleagues both in France and back in the US, who provided valuable insights and helped make the transition more manageable for him. Maintaining close connections with their friends and family in the US gave Mia the courage and inner strength to embrace her new life, and to acknowledge the fact that her husband's career was soaring while hers had been interrupted.

To prevent envy from taking a foothold in Mia's life, she proposed to her husband that he add extra monthly payments to their retirement plan and the kids' college fund, as well as directing a bigger percentage of his supplementary earnings to the family's monthly expenses to compensate for Mia's lost earnings. She also set about finding a holiday home on the French Riviera as a joint investment. In doing so, Mia chose to make the most of her time in France and temper any misgivings of having given up her career in the US. She was reassured in this by what she perceived as her husband's fair contribution to the household finances from his expat allowance. She planned to review her situation every six months, and decided that she would continue to keep her options open.

Initially hesitant, the children gradually acclimated to their new international school and surroundings. Mia and her husband prioritized their kids' integration, fostering friendships and ensuring a positive academic experience. Due to these efforts, along with their overall push for adapting better to their new circumstances, the family learned to embrace the richness of French culture, enjoying local traditions and cuisine, and forming meaningful connections with other parents at their children's school, along with their neighbors and wider community.

Mia's professional flexibility and the more adaptive mindset she had developed allowed her to flourish in her new work environment. Facing and overcoming challenges together strengthened the family's resilience, and the open communication and mutual support that they established in the US before moving to France enhanced their unity, creating a foundation for enduring success.

As the family settled into their new life in France, Mia reflected on the journey. While challenges were inevitable, the family's proactive approach, their support networks both in the US and in France, and their commitment to embracing change had resulted in a fulfilling and enriching experience. Mia found herself not only adapting to the French lifestyle but thriving in it. The family's journey highlighted the transformative power of resilience, adaptability, and a positive mindset in navigating significant life changes.

Chapter 8:

Finding Contentment and Inner Peace

Do the right thing. The rest doesn't matter. Cold or warm. Tired or well-rested. Despised or honored. —Marcus Aurelius

Living a good life is more than just good intentions. To live well, it is better to overcome the temptations of material, short-term gains and practice integrity in all interactions—but it's not always so easy! Though you always have the power to live well, the fact is that certain external events and hardships sap our spirits and lead us to make potentially bad choices.

From a cynical point of view, it may sound as though contentment and inner peace are something of a frivolous luxury. After all, you have many demands on your time and efforts. If you have a family, you have to focus on providing for them—and if providing for your children requires you to do something unfair or unjust, so be it. If you are living from paycheck to paycheck, worrying about moderation or wisdom may seem like a lofty distraction from the basic tasks of survival.

It takes strong willpower to focus on your principles instead of focusing on material concerns. It can be difficult to internalize the idea that principled living is the only path to a state of fulfilment or *eudaimonia*, both for yourself and for those you live with. However, this is what it takes.

Sam, a promising basketball senior with a bright career on the horizon, was forced to learn this the hard way when a motorbike accident left him with partial paralysis in his left leg. Basketball, which had defined much of his existence to that point, suddenly became a distant dream.

The challenge now was not only physical but also psychological, as Sam grappled with jealousy, frustration, and a need for a new sense of purpose. This understandably left him in a state bereft of contentment or inner peace, as he looked at a future that suddenly seemed incredibly dark and uncertain.

Sam was challenged on multiple fronts. Primarily, he needed to overcome the physical setback of losing the use of his left leg, which involved undergoing intense re-education to regain greater mobility. This was a painful and slow process, filled with moments when Sam's frustration overwhelmed him and caused him to wonder what the worth of his physical struggles were, since his basketball dreams had been long since destroyed.

His emotional struggles did not end there. Sam also had to cope with jealousy and resentment as he witnessed his peers pursuing their athletic endeavors, while he was forced to confront the reality of a changed, less physically fulfilling future. He was faced with the arduous task of navigating the shift in identity from a basketball-focused existence to redefining his purpose and passions in the wake of the accident.

The Pursuit of "Eudaimonia"

He who lives in harmony with himself lives in harmony with the universe. —Marcus Aurelius

Eudaimonia, or a fulfilled, flourishing life, comes from living honorably, and is nothing less than your natural state. *Eudaimonia* feels fulfilling and positive because it is living according to your core essence. It is a state of flourishing because you are living in harmony with your nature rather than pushing against it.

As a part of this view, the Stoics believed that there is a three-stage process in all human action. There is the external event that acts on you, the initial impressions you have of that external event, and then the choice of what action to take based upon the circumstances brought about by the event, how you decide to act on your impressions, and other contextual factors.

According to Stoicism, rationality lies in that third step. Animals don't have this third step, as they act on animal impulses such as hunger, fear, and anger rather than applying rationality to their "decisions." This is what elevates us as rational beings above our baser instincts, and above the status of animals. And for the Stoics, rationality and the capacity for honorable deeds are one and the same thing. Human beings are fundamentally rational, and honorable actions are always rational, so it follows that human beings are fundamentally honorable in nature.

Material goods can bring joy. There is nothing inherently wrong with gathering wealth for you and your own, or prioritizing your health. However, it is a mistake to sacrifice integrity for these goods, because this is to live in opposition to your true nature. The only *true* goods are those things that are positive in all circumstances. Other apparent goods are contextual: Wealth can lead an addict to ruin, and prioritizing yourself at the expense of others can make you a coward, leading to eventual misery. By contrast, behaving with integrity will lead you to *eudaimonia* and contentment.

Practices for Finding Contentment

It is not the man who has too little, but the man who craves more, that is poor. — Seneca

The link between *eudaimonia* and contentment is two-directional. *Eudaimonia* brings contentment, but contentment can also give you resilience against dangerous temptations. With this in mind, it can be useful to practice exercises that boost your feelings of contentment directly, and foster a mindset that can withstand life's challenges.

So, how does the achievement of *eudaimonia* and contentment through Stoicism translate into practice? Let's see how Sam began to slowly change his habits and mindset in the pursuit of his own contentment.

Recognizing the need for a change in focus, Sam underwent a profound shift in mindset. He painfully but eventually acknowledged and accepted with humility that his basketball career had taken a different trajectory, and by doing so embraced the opportunity for new beginnings. A key part of this mindset shift was the limitation of comparisons: Sam worked to focus on his unique journey and celebrate his own achievements on that journey, and slowly stopped comparing his path to that of his peers. He shut down the incessant online notifications linked to the world of basketball to protect himself from feelings of jealousy and resentment, train his mind to desire only what he could have, and make room for something new. Additionally, he focused on controlling and disciplining his desires by holding fast to the virtue of moderation through improving his self-control; this further increased his positive emotions and decreased his feelings of jealousy and resentment.

Sam decided to "circle the present," and took time to explore other passions he could engage in with his leg injury. It was by doing this that Sam discovered a love for music, and he began to immerse himself in both playing and composing it. This exploration became a therapeutic outlet and a source of joy, allowing him to redirect his energy toward a new passion.

Through the process of self-discovery and creative expression in music, Sam found a path toward inner peace. The act of creating music became a meditative practice, fostering tranquility and contentment. Sam also began to take up mindful breathing to center himself in the present moment and alleviate stress.

Sam wrote down three things that he was grateful for on a daily basis—and by doing so, cultivated a sense of gratitude for the partial recovery of his left leg and accepted the new path his life had taken. This acceptance became a cornerstone in his journey toward contentment.

When Sam thought back to that evening when he had the accident, he vividly recalled how he had been tossed over 50 meters into the air. He remembered with bitterness how the driver of the car that hit his motorbike had never even visited him in hospital or contacted him in any way, out of fear of attracting attention and a lawsuit. Despite all this, he knew with certainty that he was lucky to have escaped with his life. Feelings of gratitude and joy flooded him as he reminded himself of this many times, especially during his darkest moments. Sam made a point of anchoring his mindset to this positive perspective of his past.

He often asked himself questions to shake himself out of his depression: *Is this truly unbearable? Is this moment the one that will break me?* On reflection, he knew deep down that the answer was "no." This line of thinking always lifted his spirits and helped him switch off from agonizing about his circumstances, thereby freeing him up to engage in more meaningful activities or just switch off, take life less seriously, and simply enjoy his favorite comedy show on TV.

Recognizing the importance of a support system, Sam engaged with his family and friends, sharing his struggles and victories. Their support played a crucial role in his emotional healing. In turn, Sam himself performed small acts of kindness for others when he could, which led him to more quickly achieve a sense of fulfillment and contentment.

Some of Sam's actions were not only inspired by tenets of Stoicism, but have also been supported by years of academic study. For example, studies show that those who give more generously report happier moods (Dunn et al., 2014). Positive social interactions boost your mood and are a key predictor of well-being; evidence from studies supports a link between a positive social life and longevity (Yang et al., 2016).

Being a good person, and doing good deeds for others, feels good. By cultivating gratitude, engaging with his family and friends, and giving back to them in his own way when he could, Sam gradually found a path to the inner peace and contentment he had been sorely lacking since his accident.

Cultivating Inner Peace

He is a wise man who does not grieve for the things which he has not, but rejoices for those which he has. –Epictetus

An effective remedy for anxiety or discontentment is to visualize a place that makes you feel calm and happy. This can be a real place, or a place that exists only in your imagination. When visualizing this place, try to really inhabit it and engage all five of your senses; immerse yourself in what you see, hear, smell, taste, and feel.

Visualizing a peaceful place is calming in isolation, but it becomes an especially potent way of finding your inner peace if you visualize this place habitually. Your brain has extraordinary neuroplasticity: It strengthens those neural pathways that get more use, and weakens those neural pathways that don't. If you practice visualizing your peaceful place, you'll be able to do so more easily in the future, even in times of stress when you need it most.

Another method of achieving inner peace is spending time outside in nature. As proven by a Japanese psychological study (Lee et al., 2014), immersing yourself in nature is effective at reducing stress and boosting your psychological wellbeing. Taking walks in nature can be far more effective at reducing stress than taking walks in urban areas, so consider a trip to your local park or wood, and make nature part of your routine.

While taking these walks, other practices that boost mental well-being can be incorporated as well. For example, during walks you can focus on the beauty around you and express gratitude for your ability to experience it.

The above are just a small sample of the various practices that can help you find and maintain a robust sense of inner peace. A few others that you can adopt include the following:

Mindfulness Meditation and Practices

Practice mindfulness meditation to quiet the mind, observe thoughts without judgment, and foster a sense of inner calm. Engage in practices that combine movement and mindfulness, such as yoga or tai chi, to simultaneously promote physical and mental well-being. Practice mindful eating by savoring each bite, focusing on the sensations from your taste buds, and being fully present during meals. This helps enhance the connection between your mind and body.

Digital Detox

Take frequent breaks from electronic devices to reduce sensory and information overload and create mental space for tranquility. To aid in this, designate a peaceful corner in your home where you can unwind, read, or engage in quiet activities. As an extension of the latter point, declutter your physical and mental space. Simplifying your surroundings can contribute to an improved sense of calm and clarity.

Affirmations and Boundaries

Incorporate positive affirmations into your daily routine. Repeat phrases that promote self-love, acceptance, and inner peace. Also, learn to say no when necessary. Setting boundaries helps maintain a sense of balance and peace, and aids in the maintenance of positivity.

It is also a good idea to explore various breathwork techniques, such as 4–7–8 breathing, box breathing, or alternate-nostril breathing, to calm the nervous system. In addition, cultivate positive relationships so you can more frequently surround yourself with supportive and positive people, such as friends or loved ones, who contribute to a peaceful and uplifting environment. With them or otherwise, incorporate more humor into your day: Laughter has been scientifically proven to have therapeutic effects on both reducing stress and improving mood (Louie et al., 2016).

Engage in reading books that promote mindfulness, self-compassion, and personal growth. Take time to review and reflect on the insights you gain from them. And last but not least, prioritize quality sleep for at least six hours a night. Establish a calming bedtime routine to improve your overall well-being.

Sam: Open to New Possibilities

In the face of life's unexpected turns, our character is not defined by the road we no longer travel but by the melodies we create with the new instruments we discover. –
Unknown

Sam learned to focus on the time and opportunities he still had, and not to dwell on what might have been. He worked to make the most of his circumstances, channeling his energy into meaningful pursuits like music and embracing the opportunities for personal growth and fulfillment that still lay ahead.

Sam's focus on the possibilities and creative pursuits that arose from his accident, and the unexpected challenges that came with it, underscores the Stoic idea of adapting to circumstances and finding new avenues for personal growth and fulfillment.

Once solely defined by basketball, Sam underwent a profound transformation. While his athletic career took an unexpected turn and never approached the same peaks as before, he discovered a new sense of purpose and fulfillment through music. The cultivation of *eudaimonia*, or flourishing, became evident as Sam found inner peace, contentment, and a broader understanding of his own capabilities beyond the basketball court.

After trying a bevy of different instruments, Sam eventually found himself favoring the saxophone and other wind instruments. This in turn led him to join an amateur jazz band through some of his friends. As part of the band, Sam found himself playing at many events in his local area, a large proportion of which were in support of local initiatives to improve the quality of life in the area and other forms of community support. The sight of so many enriched and contented faces at the various events he played at contributed significantly to Sam's own sense of contentment.

Although he would never again play professionally, or even at the level he had been at before the accident, Sam eventually found the courage to pick up a basketball again and practice shots recreationally with his friends. Being able to do so without regret or a longing for what might have been was a significant milestone for him.

Sam's story illustrates the resilience of the human spirit in the face of adversity, and the potential for profound personal growth when one embraces change with an open heart and mind.

Chapter 9:

Stoic Relationships

The key is to keep company only with people who uplift you, whose presence calls forth your best. –Epictetus

Stoicism warns against staying in relationships where the other person fails to uplift you, and instead encourages you to engage in unprincipled behavior, where they hold you back when you should act with courage, or advocate selfishness when it would be better just to make amends. If you are surrounded by people like this in your life, you may find yourself picking up on their bad habits. You can become more self-absorbed and stuck in place, rather than pursuing integrity when the opportunity arises. You might complain and ruminate about the things you can't control, rather than focusing on what you can control and taking productive action.

By contrast, think about the better relationships in your life. Maybe these could be a lifelong friend, your romantic partner, or a member of your family. These people believe in you. They want you to believe in yourself and courageously strive for new opportunities. Furthermore, they hold you to account when you do something bad. They're the people in your life who'll tell you when you're in the wrong, because they know that it isn't your fundamental nature. They encourage you to be your best self and uplift you in the process.

And then there are the relationships in-between, such as those you might have with coworkers, or with friends and other associates in a recreational context; relationships come in all manner of flavors. These may not be purely detrimental nor beneficial to your life, but they are still an important part of it, insomuch as managing these relationships and the rest of your social network is vital to maintaining your mental and social health, together with your sense of perspective.

Of course, sometimes managing relationships can be difficult. If you notice that a long-term friend is holding you back and repeatedly discouraging you from doing the right thing, you might still want to hang onto the friendship for old time's sake. This isn't necessarily the wrong thing, but you need to act. Confront your friend's behavior and try to uplift *them*. Encourage them to be their best self. And, if they refuse to act with more integrity, it is wiser and fairer to yourself to distance yourself from them.

Ultimately, Stoicism advocates for holding on to your better relationships, and doing what you can to improve your worse ones. It was the latter challenge that three aspiring musicians faced when they experienced trouble with the dynamics of their band.

Emily, Malik, and Chris formed an indie band in their high school days. However, as the other responsibilities in their individual lives grew, they found it challenging to balance their personal commitments with the demands of the band. With their conflicting schedules and personal responsibilities, even the desire to find a balance between individual and band obligations became a major source of discouragement for each of the three.

The band members struggled to communicate effectively, leading to misunderstandings. Unspoken expectations fueled frustration and intolerance as each member felt the others were not committed enough to the band. All the unmet expectations and miscommunication led to a strained band dynamic, jeopardizing the harmony they once enjoyed.

Applying Stoic Principles to Relationships

Settle on the type of person you want to be and stick to it, whether alone or in company. –Epictetus

The Stoics held that the company you keep affects your own character. To some extent, this is common sense. If you surround yourself with people who are curious and inquisitive, you'll likely engage in conversations that foster your own curiosity and inquisitiveness. By contrast, if you surround yourself with people who are selfish and unreliable, chances are you'll become more selfish and unreliable yourself. The bad behavior will become normalized. With this in mind, it's important to choose your company with wisdom and care. Surround yourself with virtuous and curious people who uplift you and expect your best.

However, Stoic principles also expect you to *be* someone who uplifts the other people in your life, and this can be far more difficult to achieve. Be the person in someone's life who can hold them to account when they are doing something they'll later regret. In essence, you must *be* the kind of virtuous person you would do well to surround yourself with when deciding on the company you want to keep.

Stoicism asks you to act with integrity and honesty in your relationships. It sometimes takes courage to raise an issue that is bothering you with a friend or partner, because you may be afraid that the relationship will be compromised by you raising your concerns. However, it's important that this courage is demonstrated. A relationship that can't survive you being honest with the other person is a relationship that lacks trust. And it is very difficult for a relationship to be meaningful and successful if there is no trust between the people involved.

Like all relationships, sometimes there will be disagreements, but those disagreements will be made in good faith and with mutual respect. You will trust your friend or partner and they will trust you, because you will have always conducted yourself with integrity and fairness. Your honorable behavior will encourage them to respond in kind toward you, and vice versa. Like this, you will forge connections that will last a lifetime and help you become the best version of yourself.

The key to repairing the band dynamics between Emily, Malik, and Chris lay in the above: the application of principled thinking to their relationship with each other. Before they looked to each other, they first focused on fostering a Stoic mindset within themselves. Each band member committed to being more patient, cooperative, and understanding. They aimed to approach band matters with empathy, recognizing the challenges each of them faced.

By applying the Stoic principle of accepting the impermanence of external circumstances, the band members acknowledged that life evolves and priorities shift. This adjustment of perspective helped them adapt to the changes in their band dynamics.

Instead of fixating on external pressures, the band members focused on aspects within their control—communication, understanding, and nurturing a harmonious team spirit. Having fully accepted and understood what was required of them, they turned to each other with an eye to improve those controllable aspects of their relationships with each other.

Stoicism emphasizes the importance of thoughtful communication. The band members adopted mindful communication practices, expressing their feelings openly and actively listening to each other's concerns. Cultivating gratitude, another Stoic practice, allowed the band members to appreciate the positive aspects of their musical journey rather than dwelling on perceived shortcomings.

By adopting Stoic principles, Emily, Malik, and Chris developed a healthier communication style within the band. They expressed their musical goals and concerns openly, fostering a deeper understanding. Stoicism's focus on managing expectations helped the band members reassess and communicate their musical needs realistically. They learned to appreciate the musical journey without burdening it with unspoken expectations.

Understanding the recently imposed constraints in each other's lives, they shifted their perspective. Instead of measuring success solely in terms of time spent together, they focused on the quality of their musical interactions. Embracing the Stoic concept of adaptability, the band members developed resilience in the face of musical challenges.

Emily, Malik, and Chris's band flourished as they consciously applied Stoic principles. By embracing virtues, accepting impermanence, and focusing on what was within their control, they not only nurtured their musical collaboration but also found a deeper sense of contentment and peace within themselves. Stoicism became a guiding philosophy that strengthened their musical bond and allowed them to grow individually within the context of their shared musical journey.

Strategies for Improving Communication and Empathy

We have two ears and one mouth so that we can listen twice as much as we speak. — Epictetus

In addition to applying Stoic principles and choosing to act virtuously, there are some practical tips for improving communication and empathy in your relationships. This section will consider some of these strategies.

Active Listening

The Stoics understood that the key to good communication is listening. However, there are different kinds of listening. You can hear what someone is saying, but if you don't demonstrate that you're doing so with your body language and responses, you'll give the impression that you don't care, which is detrimental to the effectiveness of the conversation.

This is where active listening comes in. Rather than just hearing what the other person is saying, active listening involves being an active participant as a listener—showing through your body language and paralinguistic cues that you're paying attention, and asking follow-up questions that demonstrate your interest and engagement. In particular, think about the following:

Eye Contact and Body Language

Use nods and "eyebrow flashes" (brief raises of the eyebrows) to convey interest, and make sure your expression matches the tenor of the conversation. For example, when someone wants to speak to you, it is important to stop and give them your full attention rather than turning your back on them mid-sentence. Furthermore, make sure to maintain good eye contact when listening actively; this enhances trust and creates connectedness on a subconscious level.

Listening to the Unspoken Word

Hone in on listening for what the other person is *not* saying during any hesitations and pauses, as often this is the crux of the conversation rather than the words they are actually saying.

Mirroring and Asking Questions

Being a good listener isn't just about being silent and hearing what the other person is saying. It's also important to ask follow-up questions that are directly relevant to what the other person is talking about. This demonstrates to them that you are engaged and interested, and encourages them to expand on what they're talking about. In addition, mirroring or repeating back what is being said creates connection and empathy, and the other person feels heard.

Interruptions

Many people interrupt the flow of a conversation without realizing it. A remedy to this is to always wait a couple of seconds when you think someone is done talking before you say something yourself. This avoids you breaking in when someone else is merely taking a pause to gather their thoughts.

Avoiding Prejudgment

The Stoic version of justice recommends not prejudging others. It's very easy to get the wrong idea if you're prejudging what someone else is about to say. This prejudgment is also the enemy of empathy, because instead of trying to understand the other person, you are simply looking for confirmation of your own assumptions about them.

The best way to avoid prejudgment is to foster your own innate curiosity, and treat the other person as you would like to be treated. All people contain multitudes and several layers to their personalities and selves, so instead of prejudging, try to actively seek out what makes them interesting and unique. If you can foster this sense of curiosity about your conversational partner, you'll also be a better listener, because you'll be more interested in what they have to say.

Putting Yourself in Others' Shoes

Another excellent way of fostering empathy is to use Stoicism-inspired self-reflection exercises to consider the other party's point of view. First, write down your perspective of an event, thinking about the journalistic questions of what, why, when, where, and who. Then, write down another account of the same event from the perspective of the other person. Try to be charitable and avoid prejudging their motivations. Really engage your empathy, and notice how the two perspectives are different.

Putting yourself in someone else's shoes is a straightforward exercise in empathy. It's worth practicing habitually, because it trains your brain to think more naturally in an empathetic way. Through practice, your ability to see things from different perspectives will develop, and your communication skills will improve as a result.

The Band: Improved Dynamics and Preserving a Harmonious Collaboration

Harmony is not in the absence of discord, but in the deliberate composition of diverse notes, creating a symphony of resilience and shared purpose. –Unknown

By addressing their challenges head-on and navigating their conflicts with bravery, Emily, Malik, and Chris found freedom from the constraints that had hindered the band's collaboration, and were once again able to compose something beautiful together and foster harmony amid the diversity of experiences and personalities within the group.

As a result of their Stoicism and newly improved collaborative spirit, the band experienced a harmonious shift in dynamics. They navigated challenges with resilience and adapted their approach to align with their individual responsibilities.

The band's performances, though less frequent, remained successful. The inclusion of backup players ensured that they could honor their commitments to scheduled concerts, maintaining a professional standard. The band's commitment to songwriting persisted, and they consistently wrote songs that uplifted and brought brightness into their fans' lives as well as their own.

Stoicism guided them to view change as an opportunity for creative exploration, resulting in a dynamic musical repertoire that reflected their evolving perspectives. They learned to collaborate more often but remotely from their own homes, and their meetups were focused on a very specific repertoire that was decided in advance. They also made time for a get-together in the local pub after practice sessions whenever the opportunity arose.

Stoic principles allowed Emily, Malik, and Chris to grow individually within the band context as well. They recognized that personal and professional responsibilities could coexist with their shared musical journey. In addition, each member took greater ownership of specific roles in the band, like songwriting, finances, concert planning, collaborative relationships with other musicians, and ideas for new records.

In the end, the band not only weathered the challenges but flourished through mindful collaboration and a Stoic approach to change. Their musical journey became a testament to the transformative power of adapting to circumstances while remaining true to their shared passion. By prioritizing quality over quantity and embracing the evolving nature of their musical dynamics, Emily, Malik, and Chris discovered a deeper sense of contentment and fulfillment within their harmonious band.

Chapter 10:

Stoicism in the Modern World

The soul becomes dyed with the color of its thoughts. –Marcus Aurelius

The stress of the modern world encourages you to think that every decision has to be made quickly. But in doing this, you give up your rationality, because you simply act according to your immediate impressions of the situation rather than making a choice through rational thought. This is the main obstacle to integrating Stoic practices into daily decision-making. The key thing is to embrace your rationality and give yourself the time to think. Making the deliberate choice to think through a decision is half the battle; once you recognize that it's okay to not act on autopilot, you can break free of those automatic behaviors that come from immediately acting on your impulses.

Of course, this can be more difficult when you're feeling stressed or put upon. These emotions can be very insistent, pressuring you into quick reactions that are often counterproductive. This was the situation Tim found himself in when facing a typical challenge of modern life: the morning school run.

Tim was the father of two exuberant school-going children. Despite his wife's efforts to prepare everything the night before, Tim found himself consistently irritated and impatient with his kids' questions, tantrums, and demands during the daily sequence of chaotic events that took place every morning as he helped them get ready and eventually dropped them off at school. The routine would leave him feeling drained every weekday morning, which had a noticeably degrading impact on his output at his job.

This was why Tim endeavored to implement Stoic principles in his morning routine, aiming to cultivate patience, resilience, and a more tranquil morning atmosphere.

Integrating Stoic Practices Into Everyday Routines

Man conquers the world by conquering himself. –Zeno of Citium (In R. Holiday & S. Hanselman, 2016)

When Tim turned to Stoic principles to help guide his actions, he also made use of CBT techniques to improve the quality of his morning routine. As has been shown before for others, the combination of the two proved to be effective in helping him deal with his morning run troubles.

Tim began with the dichotomy of control: He recognized that he could not control his children's behavior or the unpredictable nature of the morning routine. He acknowledged, however, that his responses were within his control.

Tim embraced the Stoic idea of accepting the present moment as it is, without resisting or reacting negatively. This involved accepting the natural chaos of the morning routine with a more serene mindset, and accepting that his kids had the right to express themselves. He incorporated mindfulness techniques to stay present in the moment, letting go of anticipatory frustration or dwelling on past irritations. This allowed him to engage with his children more attentively. Tim also reminded himself to live his life with equanimity; every morning, he made it a point to maintain a calm, even-tempered mindset regardless of external circumstances.

Tim reframed his perspective by reminding himself of the bigger picture—the precious moments with his children and the value of fostering a positive relationship during the morning school run. Finally, he actively worked on cultivating patience by taking deliberate pauses, counting to 10 before responding to his children's behavior, and practicing controlled breathing to center himself. Tim applied the following techniques as well:

Cognitive Restructuring and Positive Reinforcement

Tim identified and challenged any negative thought patterns associated with the morning school run. He replaced these with more balanced and realistic ones. For example, instead of thinking, *Mornings are always chaotic*, he reframed it to, *Mornings can be challenging, but I can handle it.* Tim actively acknowledged and rewarded himself for positive behaviors during the morning routine. By reinforcing these positive actions, he strengthened desired behaviors and maintained his motivation toward continued self-improvement.

Mindfulness-Based Stress Reduction

Tim integrated mindful breathing into his morning routine to stay present in the moment. He also practiced other mindfulness exercises afterward on a regular basis, to build a foundation for greater emotional regulation. Tim practiced relaxation techniques, such as PMR or guided imagery, to manage stress and promote a calm mindset. By incorporating these techniques into his routine, together with his mindfulness exercises, he brought about a more relaxed morning atmosphere for himself.

Behavioral Activation

Tim set small, achievable goals related to his reactions during the morning routine. One such goal was to respond calmly to the first challenging situation of the day. He also hung a traffic light behavioral chart on the wall to reinforce good behavior. This chart allowed him to identify patterns, recognize improvements, and reflect on areas that potentially needed further attention both for himself and for the kids. He gradually increased the complexity of his goals to build a sense of accomplishment and reinforce positive behavior.

Problem-Solving Skills

Tim engaged in problem-solving exercises to address specific smaller challenges during the morning routine. He brainstormed various practical solutions and implemented them gradually over time. This trained him to focus on solutions rather than dwelling on problems. Tim realized that he needed to be more directive with his children rather than allowing himself to be pestered with endless questions. This enabled the kids to take more responsibility for themselves.

Prospective Retrospection

Tim visualized his kids all grown up and leaving home. He imagined feeling the sense of emptiness that would follow, and having to come to terms with an empty nest. He could see himself thinking, *Oh, why didn't I make the most of those crazy, chaotic, but wonderful days with the kids when they were young?* He suddenly felt himself overcome by sadness and regret at the thought. When Tim then returned to his kitchen with his kids rushing around, he felt an immense sense of joy, motivation, and fulfillment. He chuckled to himself as he realized this exercise was in effect an embodiment of the popular saying, "Absence definitely makes the heart grow fonder."

Graded Exposure

Certain aspects of the morning routine triggered anxiety or frustration in Tim. After actively avoiding them at first, he gradually exposed himself to these situations in a controlled and manageable way. The incremental exposure allowed Tim to build tolerance and resilience over time.

By combining Stoic principles with cognitive behavioral techniques, Tim developed a holistic approach to managing his reactions and improving the overall dynamics of the morning school run. These strategies worked synergistically to enhance his emotional resilience, promote positive thought patterns, and foster a more tranquil and fulfilling experience for both him and his family.

Tim: Being His Best Self

Amid morning chaos, a Stoic soul navigates not the absence of discord, but the mastery of its own responses, harmonizing patience and resilience to weave a more tranquil tapestry of family moments. –Unknown

When Tim began to more practically apply the principles outlined above, and in doing so set the intention to approach the morning school run with a Stoic mindset, it resulted in several beneficial manifestations of his efforts.

When faced with his children's demands, Tim refrained from reacting impulsively. Instead, he chose calm and measured responses, demonstrating to his children a more composed and Stoic approach. He also practiced mindful engagement and being fully present during the morning routine. He listened attentively to his children's questions, engaged with their conversations, and refrained from allowing anticipatory frustration to build. He also listed a set of tasks for the kids and himself for the morning routine that was visible for everyone. He set an alarm 30 minutes before leaving and another 15 minutes before leaving, by which points specific tasks were expected to be accomplished by both himself and his kids.

Tim reframed his mindset to acknowledge and accept that mornings can be inherently chaotic. Rather than resisting it, he tried to gradually embrace the unpredictability, finding peace in the knowledge that he could still control his reactions. Tim strove to consciously reinforce positive behavior in his children by acknowledging their efforts and expressing gratitude. This in turn contributed to a more harmonious morning atmosphere.

Despite Tim's efforts, challenges still arose. Some mornings were more demanding than others, and tested the limits of his resolve. Tim consistently had to remind himself that setbacks are part of the journey, and that he could use them as opportunities for self-improvement.

Even so, Tim noticed a positive shift over time in the morning school run dynamics. By implementing Stoic principles consistently, he fostered a more serene environment, cultivated a team spirit with his children, and experienced a greater sense of inner tranquility amid the morning chaos. Tim's journey serves as an example of how Stoic principles can be applied in everyday scenarios, offering ongoing guidance for personal growth and resilience.

Conclusion

Well-being is attained by little and little, and nevertheless is no little thing itself. – Zeno of Citium (In J. Holiday & S. Hanselman, 2016)

When Zeno of Citium was a pupil studying philosophy under Crates of Thebes, he showed a strong affinity for the subject, but was also overly modest and worried about how others perceived him. Crates, who followed the Cynic school of thought, saw this as a defect in Zeno and wanted to cure him of it. One day, Crates gave Zeno a pot of lentil soup to carry through a pottery district in Athens. When Zeno tried to hide the pot from view, Crates broke it with his staff, causing the lentils to spill down Zeno's legs. As he ran away in embarrassment, Crates called out after him: "Why run away, my little Phoenician? Nothing terrible has befallen you."

This lesson, from a different culture and era, was rather crude, and was intended to teach concepts from a different philosophy than Stoicism. However, there was a grain of wisdom to be found in it, which Zeno eventually incorporated into Stoic principles as well: the idea of disengaging from the immediate impressions and emotions felt when a calamitous event occurs. If Zeno had been in possession of a Stoic mindset at the time, he might have done the following instead: accept and acknowledge that there was lentil soup running down his legs, and then attempt to wipe it off or take some other remedial action that was within his ability to perform.

When my partner left me, at a time I was still shaken and reeling from the burning down of my house, I felt like running away too. And if I had, who knows where I would have ended up? Thankfully, I came across the tenets of Stoicism, not only through the words of Zeno of Citium, but also those of Marcus Aurelius, Seneca, Epictetus, and more. I acknowledged that my ashen belongings and shattered relationship were no longer within my grasp or control, and that the past was something I had to accept and live with. I was encouraged to instead be grateful for what I still possessed (my remaining friends, my bank account, and my job, among other things), and establish and work on an action plan that brought me out of my predicament, while still adhering to my core values.

It took time and effort, but the fact that I'm here, writing this book so that others may discover the same potentially life-saving truths as I did, is a testament to the fruits of my Stoic labors. This is also a key point that I want to leave you with—adopting and practicing Stoicism will require perseverance.

It's worth recognizing that the Stoic ideal is just that: an ideal. You'll fall short of those ideals every now and again, and that's acceptable. Marcus Aurelius often mentioned his own shortcomings in his book *Meditations*, demonstrating that even one of the most famous Stoics of antiquity stumbled once in a while.

When you fall short of the Stoic ideal, acknowledge the misstep, but don't seek to punish yourself through excessive guilt or self-reprimand. Such flagellation is immoderate and unjust to yourself. You cannot change how you have already acted; it is not something you can control any more. Have the courage to admit your own mistakes, but show the wisdom to learn from them too. Identify what went wrong and how you can approach similar situations in the future with more virtue. Commit to the process of becoming your best self, and recognize that every setback is an opportunity for growth.

Tips for Continued Stoic Growth

> *It's time you realized that you have something in you more powerful and miraculous than the things that affect you and make you dance like a puppet.* –Marcus Aurelius

This book has already introduced a number of Stoic principles and exercises that can fairly easily be integrated into your daily routine, such as self-reflection, mindfulness exercises, and other strategies. The more you practice these exercises, the easier it will be to think rationally in moments of stress.

This is because of the brain's neuroplasticity. The brain has the amazing capacity to strengthen neural networks that get habitual use, while letting unused neural networks naturally atrophy. If you practice thinking about impeccable action, you'll find that it becomes something you just automatically do. The key, then, is routine and habit. Persevere, keep practicing these Stoic exercises, and it will get easier to live according to the Stoic ideal:

Morning Meditation and Contemplation

Begin your day with a few minutes of mindful meditation. Reflect on Stoic principles such as acceptance of what's beyond your control and gratitude for the opportunities the day presents.

Positive Affirmations

Create Stoic-inspired affirmations focusing on virtues like wisdom, courage, justice, and moderation. Repeat these affirmations throughout the day to reinforce Stoic values together with your own core values.

Daily Reflection and Self-Examination

Maintain a daily journal where you reflect on your actions, reactions, and decisions. Ask yourself how well you embodied Stoic virtues during the day, and consider areas for improvement. Tim used a journal like this to measure his progress on how well he dealt with the morning run, as well as how well he recovered from it afterward.

Moment of Mindful Pause

When faced with challenges or stress, take a moment to pause. Reflect on the Stoic idea of responding, not reacting. Consider how you can approach the situation with integrity and rationality.

Mindful Eating and Appreciation for Simple Pleasures

During meals, appreciate the flavors, textures, and nourishment of the food you're eating. Embrace the Stoic idea of finding joy in simple, everyday experiences. In Tim's case, this also had the positive side effect of improving his relationship with his wife, who often cooked for the family.

"Premeditatio Malorum" (Preparation for Adversity)

Take a few moments to visualize potential challenges you may face in the future. This helps you mentally prepare for adversity, fostering resilience and equanimity.

Digital Detox and Detachment From External Things

Designate specific times for a digital detox. Limit exposure to external influences, focusing on inner well-being and reducing dependence on external validation. Tim spent a few hours of the day soaking in a warm bath or relaxing to soothing ambient music as a part of his own detox routine. He also returned to the gym and enjoyed relaxing in the steam room and sauna afterward—a physical detox to complement his digital one.

Kindness, Empathy, and Practicing Virtue in Relationships

Infuse acts of kindness and empathy into your day. Consider the perspectives of others and practice patience in interactions, embodying Stoic virtues in your relationships. While Tim obviously did this with his kids, he also carried the same mindset over to his interactions with others, such as his workplace colleagues.

Random Acts of Virtue

Find unplanned or unanticipated moments during the day when you can perform an act that exemplifies courage, justice, wisdom, or moderation. This helps to reinforce the habit of being virtuous.

Stoic Reading

Develop a habit of reading books that promote mindfulness, self-compassion, and personal growth. Take time regularly while reading to reflect on the insights gained. Tim discovered and then indulged an interest in multiple previously unexplored genres of literature this way.

Nightly Gratitude

Every night, write down or otherwise list three things that you are grateful for. Try to find events that occurred during the day that caused you to feel gratitude, even in a small way.

Keep persevering with the above Stoic exercises; it's important to make them part of your daily routine. The process of becoming a Stoic is tricky, requiring constant self-examination and a fair amount of grit. But, with each step you take, you'll find that living according to Stoic principles becomes easier and easier. If you keep going, one day you'll realize that you are flourishing, living in your own state of *eudaimonia*. So keep going, remain disciplined, and don't allow yourself to slack off, foster doubt, or otherwise turn from the path.

Stoicism is an ancient philosophy, but it is still of great relevance today—perhaps even more so than it has been in the recent past. By continuing to practice Stoic principles, you will remain virtuous and in control of how you respond to external events. You will have integrity, self-respect, and relationships built on mutual trust. You will build your resilience, and foster a sense of wellbeing that will change your life and empower you to reach your fullest potential.

I moved into a new permanent place about half a year after the fire. I met my current fiancé several months and many failed dates after the breakup with my ex. I was able to move on with my life and feel better than my former self within three years of the initial turmoil I suffered through. My mindset, resilience, adaptability, relationships, and overall contentment have never been better, and I have my newfound Stoic mindset and principles to thank for it.

So keep going, and may you find your own *eudaimonia* at the end of your journey into Stoicism!

Author Bio

Nikos Alexandros draws inspiration from the timeless wisdom of Stoicism in navigating the complexities of the modern world. Born into a family with a rich history of philosophical pursuits, Nikos brings a contemporary perspective to ancient philosophies. With a background in business and a passion for personal development, Nikos advocates for the practical application of Stoic principles in everyday life. In a fast-paced and ever-changing society, he believes in the enduring relevance of Stoicism, guiding individuals toward inner resilience, emotional intelligence, and virtuous living. As a modern Stoic, Nikos encourages readers to embrace the philosophy as a powerful tool for thriving in turbulent times.

References

Aurelius, M. (2006). *Meditations* (M. Hammond, Trans.). Penguin Classics. Original work published 161–180.

Bobzien, S. (1998). *Determinism and freedom in Stoic philosophy*. Clarendon Press.

Bushman, B. J. (2002). Does venting anger feed or extinguish the flame? Catharsis, rumination, distraction, anger, and aggressive responding. *Personality and Social Psychology Bulletin, 28*(6), 724–731. https://doi.org/10.1177/0146167202289002

Center for Creative Leadership. (n.d.). *How to set achievable goals (that align with your values)*. https://www.ccl.org/articles/leading-effectively-articles/achievable-personal-goals-align-with-values/

Christoph, J. (2009). *Stoic virtues: Chrysippus and the religious character of Stoic ethics*. Continuum Publishing Corporation.

Cote, C. (2022, March 10). *Growth mindset vs. fixed mindset: What's the difference?* Harvard Business School Online. https://online.hbs.edu/blog/post/growth-mindset-vs-fixed-mindset

Digiuseppe, R. A., Doyle, K. A., Dryden, W., & Backx, W. (2013). *A practitioner's guide to rational-emotive behavior therapy*. Oxford University Press. https://doi.org/10.1093/med:psych/9780199743049.003.0001

Dunn, E. W., Akin, L. B., & Norton, M. I. (2008). Spending money on others promotes happiness. *Science, 319*(5870), 1687–1688. https://doi.org/10.1126/science.1150952

Dunn, E. W., Akin, L. B., & Norton, M. I. (2014). Prosocial spending and happiness: Using money to benefit others pays off. *Current*

Directions in Psychological Science, 23(1). https://doi.org/10.1177/0963721413512503

Epictetus. (2008). *Discourses and selected writings* (R. Dobbin, Trans.). Penguin Classics. Original work published c.108.

Hame, S. L. (2023, January 25). *6 cold shower benefits to consider.* UCLA Health. https://www.uclahealth.org/news/6-cold-shower-benefits-consider

Holiday, R., & Hanselman, S. (2016). *The daily Stoic: 366 meditations on self-mastery, perseverance and wisdom.* Penguin Publishing Group.

Irvine, W. B. (2019). *The Stoic challenge: A philosopher's guide to becoming tougher, calmer, and more resilient.* W. W. Norton & Company

Laertius, D. (1925). *Diogenes Laertius: Lives of eminent philosophers* books 1–5. (R. D. Hicks, Trans.). Harvard University Press. Original work published c.1472.

Lebow, H. I. (2022, May 17). *Adapting to change: Why it's important and how to do it.* PsychCentral. https://psychcentral.com/blog/adapting-to-change

Lee, J., Tsunetsugu, Y., Takayama, N., Park, B.-J., Li, Q. Song, C., Komatsu, M., Ikei, H., Tyrväinen, L., Kagawa, T., & Miyazaki, Y. (2014). Influence of forest therapy on cardiovascular relaxation in young adults. *Evidence-Based Complementary and Alternative Medicine.* https://doi.org/10.1155/2014/834360

Louie, D., Brook, K., & Frates, E. (2016). The laughter prescription: A tool for lifestyle medicine. *American Journal of Lifestyle Medicine, 10*(4), 262–267. https://doi.org/10.1177/1559827614550279

M. K. (2023). *The big book of Friedrich Nietzsche quotes.* Independently published.

Oppland, M. (2023, October 3). *13 most popular gratitude exercises & activities.* PositivePsychology.com. https://positivepsychology.com/gratitude-exercises/

Ovid. (2008). *Metamorphoses*. (A. D. Melville & E. J. Kenney, Trans.). Oxford University Press. Original work published 8.

Richo, D. (2002). *How to be an adult in relationships: The five keys to mindful loving*. Shambhala Publications Inc.

Seneca, L. (2018). *Letters from a stoic: The 124 epistles of Seneca – complete* (R. M. Gummere, Trans.). Lulu.com. Originally written c.65.

Sun, J., Harris, K., & Vazire, S. (2020). Is well-being associated with the quantity and quality of social interactions? *Journal of Personality and Social Psychology, 119*(6), 1478–1496. https://doi.org/10.1037/pspp0000272

Yakusheva, O., Kapinos, K. A., & Weiss, M. E. (2011). Peer effects and the freshman 15: evidence from a natural experiment. *Economics & Human Biology, 9*(2), 119–132. https://doi.org/10.1016/j.ehb.2010.12.002

Yang, C. Y., Boen, C., Gerken, K., Li, T., Schorpp, K., & Harris, K. M. (2016). Social relationships and physiological determinants of longevity across the human life span. *The Proceedings of the National Academy of Sciences, 113*(3), 578–583. https://doi.org/10.1073/pnas.1511085112

Printed in Great Britain
by Amazon